*Initiative*

Janie Poo you are
My favorite !
12/30/11

By

Greg S. Reid

SHERPA
press

*Initiative* by Greg S. Reid
Copyright © 2011 by Greg S. Reid

Sherpa Press
2510 Warren Ave Suite 3898
Cheyenne, WY 82001
*www.sherpapress.com*

ISBN 978-0-9829850-3-8
Library of Congress Cataloging Data

The following authors have generously granted permission to use extended quotations of their works: *Better, Faster and Different* by Harry Paul. *The Power of Initiative* by Brian Tracy. *Take A Chance* by Ruben Gonzalez.

# Initiative

By

**Greg S. Reid**

## Appreciation

In addition to Summer Felix, special thanks and acknowledgement go out to all the leaders and dreamers who make this world a better place. They are always examples of service!


## Introduction

Over the centuries, lessons have best been absorbed through parables and stories passed along from one generation to the next. This book continues that tradition with a modern-day tale that reinforces the strategies for personal and business success that have stood the test of time.

Throughout these pages, you will be reminded of age-old wisdoms, which may rekindle the entrepreneurial spirit that made this nation so great and that lies within you, ready to be shared with the world.

Enjoy and whatever you do.... Keep smiling!

# Contents

# *Foreword*

During these unstable, turbulent and unpredictable times we're facing, people need a tried and true method that will ensure they can live their dreams, rebuild their lives and become financially secure. Greg Reid, talented author, dynamic speaker and personal empowerment guru challenges all of us to stop whining, blaming and being frightened out of our wits, and take the initiative to create a new reality for ourselves.

This book was written for you to live your life from a place of power. When you use your power within you to take the initiative, rather than sit around and complain about the government or the economy, your life begins to improve instantly. Initiative requires vision, courage and action. These are the primary ingredients for living a meaningful, significant and extraordinary life. This book contains stories, insights and wisdom that will give you major breakthroughs in every area of your life.

In today's world, initiative is the master key required to reinvent yourself, expand your vision and take charge of your destiny. The dictionary defines initiative as, "readiness to embark on a bold adventure." By applying the principles in each chapter, your life will soar to new heights. Every new discovery, innovation or invention came about because somebody took the initiative to invest the time, energy and effort to make it a reality.

What is your dream? Whatever it is, don't take it to your grave. Use this book as your tool to conquer your fears, overcome procrastination, and live the life you envision by taking the initiative. It's in your hands now. You're being given the master key.

Les Brown
Motivational Speaker, Author

Live Your Dreams
It's Not Over 'til You Win
Up Thoughts for Downtimes
Fight for Your Dreams

*If you aren't fired with enthusiasm,*
*you will be fired with enthusiasm.*

— Vince Lombardi

# Chapter 1

# KNOW WHERE TO GET YOUR FUEL
# APPRECIATE THE CLUES

On some level, she always assumed one-day she would exceed what everyone else thought she was merely capable of doing. She knew the day would come when she would stop biting her nails, stop driving by the gym only to turn around and go home, stop buying gifts for birthday parties and then not going and stop believing every negative thing her mother said. One day, she would smile more times than not, she'd watch more comedies, she'd go out on a date and she'd actually commit to the commitments she made.

Now, on a good day, it feels like she's in a JC Penny catalogue surrounded by trying-to-be-chic-thirty-somethings, smiling cheerfully as if they are actually really happy with their lives. Whether they are or not, doesn't really matter, at least they are being polite.

On a normal day, they aren't smiling, just like her, and she hangs her head low because she's nearly a decade older than most of them and still questioning whether her life is already over or just nearing the end. It was getting hard to tell.

"Morgan Kingsbury?"

The phone system had been untouched since the early 90s and caused everyone a punch of adrenaline every time the buzzer went off.

"That's me."

"It's Rachel from HR."

"Uh huh."

"We'd like to see you in a half-hour."

"No problem." Morgan's voice tried its best to match the good day cheery smiles, but clearly, practice was not making perfect.

She knew this day was coming. She was never satisfied with this job. It didn't bring her any joy, except for the occasional heart-warming thank-you notes from the recently employed, courtesy of Morgan herself. She was pretty good at it and it came easy to her. She had the skills to negotiate good salaries and benefits for her clients and the companies she provided staffing for never sent a single complaint. Her ten plus years at Superior Staffing were about to bring her a promotion. On the one hand, it was nice to be appreciated and while she didn't do too much with her free time, the extra money wouldn't hurt. The only downside to this promotion was that she wasn't going anywhere. At this company, the road would stop.

She glanced at the clock and then at her desk. She looked over to her left at Alicia's desk and contemplated the new family picture that was just put out. The baby looked about a year old now. She scanned the rest of Alicia's grey corkboard and faux wall. They seemed happy in their pictures. They went to Tahiti for their honeymoon. He proposed on the beach. Their wedding was at a vineyard and she seems to have lost all the baby weight since delivery. Each picture told the story that every girl wished. Alicia also took great pride in her work and Morgan imagined her parents and in laws would sing her praises for being an attractive, good mother who could work and manage it all. She got really excited with every new client she found a job for and here was Morgan, completely void of any of those emotions. She had no children. She wasn't married. She was never proposed to and Tahiti was something that would probably never happen.

She took a breath and sighed out the rest of the air. It was time to walk downstairs to HR and accept a promotion for something which she has no passion for. But, then again, maybe that was all life was supposed to be. Maybe she should be happy to have some sort of security and parents to pat her on the back for a job well kept.

Walking into Rachel's office, she smelled the burning butterscotch candle mixed with re-heated Chinese leftovers.

An almost empty plate sat just behind Rachel with a fork still plowed into the noodles. The food looked good to Morgan, but even more so was the thought of what Rachel might have brought for dessert. Morgan included dessert for every meal, outside of breakfast. Instead, she'd have dessert in lieu of the recommended first meal of the day. Her mouth started to water. It was a little something that made her heart beat just a little faster.

"Hi, Morgan. How are you?" Rachel was always very proper regardless of the issue that needed to be discussed. Morgan nodded and took her seat pulling in the vision of the diploma Rachel proudly placed on the wall just behind her chair. Morgan pictured Rachel at the University of Notre Dame in high-waisted jeans and a plaid shirt rushing to get to her classes for the fear of looking rude or irresponsible.

"All is good on my end. How are you?"

Ignoring Morgan's response, Rachel swiveled her chair and grabbed a file and turned back to face Morgan. "As you may be aware, Superior Staffing is in the process of making changes. We've had to give more responsibility to some, while letting others go. It's the way of the business and it's my responsibility to manage such changes." She paused and squinted her blue eyes to read Morgan's face. "Are you with me?"

"Absolutely." Morgan waited for her new list of responsibilities and assured herself that the extra pay would be worth it. She continued to eye Rachel's desk for a hint of pastry, chocolate or even better, a cupcake.

"Unfortunately, Morgan, you are one of the staff members we will be letting go."

Morgan's wandering eyes were immediately brought to focus on Rachel's mouth. Her usually pleasant face that complimented her naturally curly brown hair, twisted into something unrecognizable.

She cleared her throat. "I'm sorry?"

"It really has nothing to do with your performance Morgan and more to do with your enthusiasm." She paused. "Well, your deficiency of enthusiasm."

Morgan started to chew her nails and crinkled her nose even more while trying to absorb the words. Suddenly, a cupcake didn't sound so good and the scent of Chinese food was making her queasy.

"Okay...."

Rachel tilted her head as if to offer some sort of compassion. "It seems you're not happy here and Superior Staffing is about encouraging our clients to be employed." Morgan didn't receive the hint of compassion. Rachel tilted her head upright again. "You understand, right?"

Wow. Was it that obvious? And wait. What? Was she really getting fired because she wasn't excited about filing paperwork for an out-of-work mailroom assistant? The feeling of nothingness and shock suddenly turned to anger and finally into a last attempt to save her unfulfilling job. The worst of it all? What would her mother say?

"Is there someone I can talk to? I mean is Josh or Paul around? It just seems unfair that you would fire me just because this isn't my dream –"

"Morgan, the company is going through reorganization. It's nothing personal – "

"But it feels personal. If I'm doing a good job then why are you letting me go?"

She fought for a bit longer. But, even with the protest, the excitement for the job never came through and it was obvious, even to her, that it was time for her to move on. But, what would be next? What would she do now?

How did she suddenly go from being disinterested in a promotion to suddenly becoming unemployed at 42, with two weeks severance pay and two parents she still had to answer to?

There was only one place that could bring any light of happiness to her sullen mood – Café la Claire. It was the one coffee shop that she always loved to visit to just watch people, but there was never enough time. Instead she would grab her morning java at any old drive-through franchise and then rush to make her daily 8:00 AM staff meetings. That was over now. Tomorrow, she could sleep in. She could even sit down and get coffee and a dessert from the bakery bar and do absolutely nothing. A small smirk on her face crept up as she fantasized about the next morning. Maybe this wouldn't be so bad.

Unfortunately, sleeping in was not a success. The first hint of sunlight woke Morgan up as usual. Her eyes would often open just before the alarm went off each morning, and this morning was no different, except that she now had nowhere to be. Life was at a standstill and she didn't have much time to figure out what lay ahead. What she did know was that a chocolate éclair and sweetened cappuccino awaited her at Café la Claire.

"Morgan," the barista called out.

Morgan got up and grabbed the alluring éclair and hot drink and appreciated the hand-painted ceramic cup as she found a cozy table in the corner of the shop.

She looked around the cottage-style café and back at her dessert. For a moment, she considered that this might be the first time she was smiling out of pure enjoyment. She took her first bite, and then another. She followed the second bite with a careful sip of cappuccino and took a deep breath as it all made its way to her tummy. She closed her eyes for just a few delectable seconds. She felt content, at least for the moment.

Bzzz. Bzzz. Bzzz. Her cell phone started to vibrate in her purse. She fumbled around and tried to grab it as the vibrations were disrupting her brief moments of bliss. She grasped everything but the phone, until finally her fingers clenched the demanding electronic device and she answered. "Hi, it's Morgan."

"Morgan, it's me."

She looked at her phone and confirmed that yes, it was "me", that is, her mother.

Sounding less than enthused, "Yeah, hi Mom."

"You sound irritated. Are you?"

"No, Mom, I'm fine. Just having an éclair and cappuccino at Café la Claire. You know I've always wanted to have a day in the middle of the week, where I could just – "

"Café what? What are you doing there? Why aren't you at work?"

"La Claire, Mom. Café la Claire. You know that little French country-style coffee shop on the corner of Brand and Stinson?"

"No. No, I don't. Why aren't you at the office? Is something wrong?"

"Um, well, I'm not actually working at Superior Staffing anymore."

"Ha ha. Very funny, Morgan. What kind of promotion did they offer you?"

Morgan's heart started to beat faster and her lips were starting to grit. She looked at her chewed up fingernails. "No, Mom. There was no promotion. They actually let me go."

"Morgan, will you stop? It couldn't have been that bad. Any raise is better than no raise and it's a tough economy right now. Did you try to negotiate?"

"Mom!" She started to yell now. A few people surrounding her took notice. She quickly lowered her voice into the phone. "There was no raise. There was no negotiating. They're downsizing or restructuring or something like that. All I know is I got fired. They let me go. I have two weeks severance and a referral if I need it."

There was silence on the other end of the line.

"Mom?"

"After ten years, they fire you? After all you've done for them. What was the problem? Were you employing the wrong people? I thought you had a good record with the clients. That's what you told me anyway."

Morgan's breath became audible now.

"Were they unhappy with your communication skills? You know you could stand to be sweeter on the phone."

This was typical, Morgan thought. She knew her mother would find out. It was just the beginning of the decline in self-esteem she was already feeling. It was bad enough that her parents would be disappointed that she couldn't stick to her mundane, low-paying job or get even a smidge of a promotion, but on top of that, now her mom told her that she couldn't even give good phone.

"It wasn't my performance per se." She tried to soften the situation, but she could feel her mother's condemning opinion darting through the phone as if she had anticipated this day all along.

"Well, then?"

It was as if she was sixteen again and she failed her algebra test and had no justifiable answer as to how this could have happened after four hours a week of paid tutoring. "Look, Mom. I'm going to hang up now."

Getting in the last word, her mother said, "Your father and I paid good money for you to go to an established university. Your sister became partner in less than three years and makes bonuses bigger than your salary. She's thirty-four. You find a job, Morgan. You start looking. I'll do what I can to place you somewhere."

Ha! Now, her mom would be her staffing agent. Morgan knew which jobs were available. She had access to the lists every day. There wasn't much that would match her salary, outside of folding clothes and serving tables with good tips. But she hung up the phone and grabbed the town's local paper that sat stacked just beside the bakery bar and remembered why she couldn't attend her nephew's fourth birthday. She searched her purse again for a pen until she finally found one. As she opened it, the ink splattered everywhere. Great. Just what she needed. Her half-eaten éclair was losing its appeal and the cappuccino was even less exciting. The buzz of her pseudo day off was killed by that last phone call. She grabbed an eyeliner pencil from her make-up bag and started to peruse the classifieds for another ordinary job.

However, the more she looked, the more distracted she got. Every time she read the descriptions of the "opportunities" available, her stomach would drop at the idea of sitting at another desk job and having to wake up the same time every morning for something that gave her no thrill. She continued to circle those she might have a chance at getting and then looked around the cafe. She couldn't help but feel as if the people here were living in a different world than she . She watched their smiles and the extra spring in their movements. She started to feel as if she was living in a bubble that no one else could see, as if she was completely separate from the rest of those walking around her. But, she wanted so desperately to be a part of their world. What was it that motivated them to wake up? What drove them? What was their initiative?

She continued to watch each person as they placed their orders, sat at tables, conversed with their friends, played with their children, rubbed noses with their spouses, brainstormed business ideas and just smiled. If only she could be part of it.

Amid the absorbing of painful happiness surrounding her, she heard her phone again. Without looking she picked it up again, assuming it was her mother. "Yeah?" she answered.

"Well, you must be in a good mood." A man on the other end responded.

Morgan laughed feeling a little embarrassed, "Dan, I'm sorry."

"No, it's fine. I guess I should have expected it. I heard what happened." His voice was echoing.

"Already?" She was confused.

"Yeah, I'm actually sitting right behind you."

Morgan looked behind her and sure enough there was Dan. She didn't know how she could have missed him. His broad shoulders and fit physique doesn't go unnoticed by anyone. She shook her head to her own dismay and ended the call. Dan walked over to Morgan and sat down.

"What's up?" Dan Kravitz had a cool way about him that set people at ease.

"I'm actually really happy you're here." She looked around, "And I have no idea how I didn't see you there."

"I have my subtle ways," he smiled.

"So, yeah, I lost my job." Morgan hung her head low. While she felt as such each with Dan, she still felt embarrassed telling someone like him she failed. He was a longtime friend of Morgan's and she noticed herself pulling away as he grew to be more successful. He knew this and called her out on it a few times. But, she would always defend herself with the busyness of her life, which wasn't true in the slightest and Dan knew this.

"Well, congratulations!" Dan beamed back to Morgan.

"Really? That's what you're going to say?"

"Every time I failed, something better came along."

"Yeah, I know they say that, but how can that be when I feel so down?"

"Because now is the time you need to give more. That's when doors start to open. You can climb out of this one, Morgan. Heck, you can climb out of anything. I know you can. I just don't know that you know." Dan took a sip of his hot drink.

"I feel like I'm missing something. You know that gene or whatever it is that all these people," she motioned around the café, "seem to have and especially you, Mr. Kravitz. You never seem to falter."

"We all falter, Morgan. But, you have to have the courage to step out in front of the parade." He let her marinate in that for a moment before continuing. "See, where most people just survive, I want to thrive and I think you're reaching the point of realizing that's what you want too."

"What do I do?" Morgan asked.

"Be a leader in a world full of followers. That's what I did. I decided that I could wait forever for something to show up or I could make it happen myself. I could create my own opportunities."

"You've been trying to tell me this for a long time, haven't you?" Morgan questioned with a smirk.

Dan smiled back, "You knew all along, I'm just reinforcing it at the time you're ready to hear it."

"What's my first step?"

"Simple."

"Tell me!"

"Know where you get your fuel." Dan was flat with his answer and firm. He waited for the light bulb to go off in Morgan's head.

Morgan kept looking at him, her brows furrowed in thought. Dan looked at a magazine that was sitting next to Morgan. "What's that?" he asked.

Morgan looked over and picked it up as if it was obvious. "You know, just a tabloid magazine."

"Stimulating?" Dan raised his eyebrows knowing the obvious answer.

Morgan laughed, "Oh I get it." She looked it over. "Well, I for one want to know about Jen's wedding and how much her dress was."

Dan laughed with Morgan. "But, you're right. I waste a lot of time on this stuff and it's really not all that stimulating at all."

"Know where to get your fuel." He said it again and this time Morgan got the point. "I gotta run. But, keep in touch. Let me know how things go for you. I'm just a call away."

"I will." Morgan agreed and then, "Hey, Dan?" Dan started to leave but looked back. "Thank you and... I'm sorry." He knew what she meant and he accepted it with a warm smile.

Morgan's attention turned back to the café and the patrons she was previously engaged in. As she watched them all, one woman in particular came into focus. She was alone. She wasn't speaking to anyone. She just sat by herself, completely content reading a book. There was so much activity going on in the café, so many interactions and so much energy and this one woman seemed to embrace it all. She, like Morgan, was the only other one alone in the shop and yet she seemed to be a part of the life that was happening, while Morgan felt so isolated from it all. She looked down at her classifieds again and felt as if she wanted to tear it all up. "I'm done with this."

She stood up and walked over to the dark haired woman who happily sat with her book and tea.

"Excuse me." Morgan said nervously.

"Hi," the woman said.

"I'm sorry to disturb you, but I couldn't help notice…," she paused, searching for the proper words.

The woman waited and then, "Yes?"

"Well, it's just that…"

Looking around for confirmation, "Yes?"

Morgan cut to the point. "You seem so content."

The woman smiled and chuckled a little bit. "Thank you. You're right – I am content, but that's because I only do things that I love to do."

That simple idea struck Morgan and she wanted so badly to sit down with this woman that she'd known for only seconds. The woman still smiled and watched Morgan and observed her thinking. "What is it that you love to do when you don't have to be doing anything else?"

Morgan laughed. "Um." She couldn't come up with an answer. The truth was she didn't remember ever doing something that she didn't have to do. Except for right now. "Oh. Well, I guess I like to eat pastries and sip cappuccinos."

"Well, there you go. That's a start."

Morgan absorbed this for a moment. "What do you do? I mean what is it that you do that makes a total stranger like me want to come up and talk to you?" She laughed nervously, realizing how absurd she must appear to this woman, let alone how crazy she appeared to herself.

"May I ask your name?" The woman didn't seem to notice any hint of foolishness.

"I'm Morgan," relieved at her acceptance.

"Morgan, have a seat. I'm Donna Beccia," She gestured to the available chair and then gave Morgan the same hand to shake. Morgan firmly grasped her hand and returned the introduction. "What is it you're looking for?"

Morgan searched for something. "The sad part is, I don't even know." Donna waited for more, or at least that's what Morgan thought she was doing. "I mean really. I just don't know. I just want to feel… excited about something I guess."

"That's great." Donna was quick to respond and Morgan was confused.

"It is?"

"Absolutely." Donna had a really soft smile that warmed Morgan and also made her feel compelled to learn more.

"But, how do I figure out what that is?"

"That's easy. When you have nothing else to do, what do you do when no one is looking? That's what you love to do." Donna told Morgan. Morgan had to think about this for a minute. And then she knew exactly what she did or would want to be doing. But, it felt so foolish to her. She actually felt embarrassed thinking of it and she hadn't said anything yet.

"You don't have to share the information with me. Just know it for yourself right now." It was as if Morgan's face was displaying words and Donna was reading them. "What do you have in there?" Donna pointed to Morgan's purse.

"Oh." Morgan laughed. "Probably a bunch of stuff I don't really need."

"Do you carry a calendar and checkbook with you?" Donna continued.

"Um, well, I have everything on my phone. Calendar, banking..."

"When you get home tonight, take a look at your calendar and checkbook, and also your collection of books. Your calendar will tell you what you're spending your time on. Your checkbook will show what you spend your money, what you consider valuable. And your books and magazines will reveal what you're spending your mind on. These are your priorities. These are clues to what is important to you. When you are doing what is passionate to you, it's easy to smile and feel a sense of purpose about your life."

The idea of looking into her life and what she spent time on was terrifying to Morgan. But, it was also oddly exciting.

One part of her wanted to delay the night from ever coming and the other part couldn't wait to get home and review the contents of her purse, her calendar, her checking account, and her books.

Donna looked over at Morgan's éclair and smiled. "Those are delicious, aren't they?"

Morgan's face lit up almost immediately. "Probably one of my favorites." Suddenly her appetite was back.

Donna stood up and collected her bag and book. "I should really go now."

"I hope I haven't disturbed your day." Morgan felt awful for having barged in on this woman's alone time.

"You haven't disturbed me at all. I enjoyed what I was doing before you approached me, and I enjoyed talking to you. That's my life goal – to do what I love and to love what I'm doing."

Morgan stood up to thank her again for her time. But before she could say anything, Donna took Morgan's hands in her own and whispered, "Appreciate the clues." She turned and left.

Thoughts flooded Morgan's mind as she walked up to her apartment door and searched for the keys that floated around in her big handbag. She opened the door and sat down on her worn couch. She looked around and noticed her bookshelf that displayed only a few good reads. She sat up a bit more and noticed her walls. The portraits hanging on the walls made her smile, especially the ones she picked herself. She frowned at the ones her mother handed down to her. She thought back to when she purchased those prints of the quaint French cafés that lined the streets of Paris. She smelled the *café au lait* that sat on the wrought iron bistro sets. The painted steam was so intricate in the painting; it was enough to tickle her nose. And the croissants. She smiled as she thought about biting into the perfectly detailed croissant held by the dark-haired woman in the portrait.

She walked over to her kitchen to find something to eat. It had been some time since she enjoyed that éclair and the paintings were doing an excellent job of revving her cravings. On her way to the fridge, she noticed that her purse had been sitting on the counter. The zipper was opened and it was bursting with 'stuff', the stuff she was encouraged to look at. Earlier, there was a hint of an excitement to rush home and view her life as it stood now. Right now, the fear of this revelation was overshadowing the adventure of it all. But, she made a promise to herself and to Donna that she would do this. "Appreciate the clues," Donna told her. And now, the clues were being given. Morgan knew this, but it was up to her to accept them. The self-test was about to begin, with the examination of an untidy handbag.

She picked up the leather creation and perched it upright. She reached in and looked at the first thing. It was a pen from Superior Staffing. She set it aside and reached for something else. But, before pulling it out, she dropped it back inside the purse and took the whole bag and spontaneously dumped it onto the counter.

"This is a mess, a complete boring, unexciting mess," Morgan thought. There were crumpled up receipts, coins that would probably add up to about five dollars at least, a leaking tube of lip gloss, wadded up gum wrapped inside a piece of napkin, a debit card, an old grocery list, a hairbrush filled with too much hair, extra keys that were a mystery, a half-eaten candy bar that she had forgotten to finish. Laying there next to her fingerprint-covered phone was a bottle of headache medicine of which had become more of a daily supplement for her than occasional relief. She took her phone and walked back to the couch to open up the calendar. Only a few days of the month, she had something to do other than to go to work. Her calendar verified that she missed her cousin's baby shower and her nephew's birthday party. The coupon for a free yoga class had now expired, and she didn't do that either. "Appreciate the clues," she could hear Donna's whispered words. According to her calendar and purse, her days were filled with chewing gum and headaches. What were the clues telling her? Get a life!

Now, was as good a time as any to throw away some of this crumpled paper from her purse. She took the wrinkled papers and combined them into a ball for a swift swoop into the garbage can.

Next, Morgan decided to review her receipts. What exactly was she spending her treasure on? She opened the first receipt and then the next. She put them side by side.

*Pain au Chocolate* (1)...... $2.50
*Profiterole* (3).......$1.75 each
*Beignet* (2).........$3.25 each
*Croissant Amande* (1).......$2.50
*Madeleines* (2 bags).......$1.25 each
Chocolate Covered Macaroon (1)...... $2.25
Assorted Cupcakes (1 Dozen)......$11.75

"Wow," she thought. With each receipt, she remembered the time and place that she ate them. She never sat to enjoy them, but bought them and took them to her desk, where she would briefly fantasize of a more preferred whereabouts as she ate them. It seemed like every lunch break included a visit to the closest grocery store or bakery to try out such sweet delights. Her grocery lists had very little to do with the basics like meat, veggies, breads or dairy. Instead they were filled with recipe ingredients.

1 bag All Purpose Flour
2 lbs brown sugar
Baking powder
Eggs
Milk
Vanilla Extract
Butter.

Every item she looked at made her smile. There was something special about buying all of these ingredients, taking them home, laying them out on the counter with the mixing bowls, the stirring utensils, the electronic beaters, the whisks, the pans, the frosting . . . Oh, the frosting. Morgan especially enjoyed turning on the oven and then feeling the heat as it warmed her cold toes. She was quite good at cake decorating too.

Morgan often turned down invitations to attend social events, responding with an apology and a delivery of homemade sweet breads, cupcakes or cookies, all decorated with an appropriate theme. She would often get thank-you notes, encouraging her to start her own baking business.

"These are fabulous! We are so sorry you were ill and couldn't join us. I think you have a calling with your baking!"

Every once in a while she would remember the criticism from her mother, who insisted that baking was a juvenile and a hobby, not something to turn into a career. Her enthusiasm fire would quickly be extinguished by the disapproval of her mother. So, the would-be baking career remained a hobby and Morgan felt guilt about that.

As the night continued on, the apartment filled with the smell of freshly baked *brésiliennes,* and Morgan realized, for the first time, that these were the moments that made her feel happy, peaceful, and excited all at the same time. She curled up on the couch with one petite four and a blanket and dozed off after the first bite.

# Chapter 2

# THE PROMISSORY NOTE
# BETTER, FASTER, DIFFERENT

In her forty-two years of life, Morgan was never one to follow through with the commitments she made to herself or to others. She did what she absolutely had to do to get her paycheck and keep the peace. But, it was quickly becoming clear that this wasn't proving to be a beneficial thing. Where exactly was her life headed? The contents of her purse were making it painfully obvious.

When Morgan considered her encounter with Donna at Café la Claire, she questioned which was more important – happiness or the initiative to be happy? Why wasn't she experiencing either of these?

She was still in need of a job, but she wasn't anywhere ready to tackle a job search today. Baking was the one thing that added a spring to her step, so Morgan decided to go out and get more ingredients. The day was warm and she was spending entirely too much time with her legs crossed underneath a desk. So, today she decided she to walk the streets of this somewhat urban town and let the sun hit her pale skin.

She took her purse and sunglasses and headed out. Before picking up baking supplies she decided to stop at the newsstand to pick up some reading material for her pleasure. "Become the Owner of Your Life" was what one of the articles was titled. "Hmph, I wish." She said outwardly.

"One of those days?" The owner was standing right next to her and she barely noticed until he spoke.

"Oh, sorry, I must have been speaking out loud." She apologized.

"Don't be sorry. But, just know, nothing bad lasts forever."

"What if it felt like forever?" She said, laughing, but mostly serious.

"Well, you may not have the knowledge right now to get out of something bad or start something good, but you definitely have the resources." He looked around him.

"I guess so." She still wasn't offering her full attention and let her mind drift into pictures of women in next season's fashion and headlines of the latest affair.

She read headline after headline until she suddenly stopped and looked up at the stranger. She felt immediately mortified that she had just glued her eyes to a gossip magazine. "Yikes." She left a few bucks on the stand and took the original magazine encouraging her to own her own life.

Dan was right. What was she spending her mind on? Which parts were actually attributing to her life? And which parts were actually wasting her time?

On her way to her favorite culinary supply store, she noticed a small shop she hadn't seen before. The storefront displayed beautiful pyramids of canned tea, each with a unique photo and message. The day was warm, but not too warm for tea.

Upon entering the store, she could feel a sense of well-being all around. It was a feeling she could stand to have a lot more often. She read the labels of each tea and smelled the samples laid out.

"Thank you, Louise! We'll see you next time." The man behind the counter waved to a woman just leaving. He came out from behind the counter to reorganize some displays and offered Morgan assistance.

"I'm just looking. I'd love a cup now, though." Morgan requested from the kind man. She couldn't help but smile when she looked at him. He seemed to have an agreeable grin whether he was interacting with someone or not.

"Any in particular or shall I surprise you?"

"Um, well I was never one for surprises, so I'll say yes to that!" They both laughed and he went forward with preparing the tea. "What's your favorite?"

"Peace of Mind." He didn't hesitate.

"Sounds good to me!" She made one more round before walking up to the counter to collect her cup of tea and Peace of Mind tea to go. As he rang up her purchases, she viewed the wall just behind him. It was covered with hundreds of notes and letters glued to the wall, all signed by James Pham. She couldn't help but ask, "May I ask what all those notes are?"

He smiled right away. "Those are my promissory notes."

She didn't understand. "Excuse me?"

"Promissory notes. I wrote them to everyone I knew and I promised each individual to be a success and once I was I would share with them."

"Wow."

"Talk about being accountable." He laughed.

"I'll say." She wasn't finished there yet. "How did you come up with that idea?"

"Sometimes you reach a point where nothing is going the way you want. Things got pretty bad before I finally decided what I wanted to do with my life. But, it would never happen if I didn't have the support of these 275 people." He pointed to the wall. By making the promise to them, I made the commitment with myself."

Morgan nodded.

"I wrote a letter to every person I knew and asked for help."

"Scary." Morgan couldn't imagine doing something like that. Who did she know any way that would support her?

"Yeah, but sometimes you get to the point, where the fear just doesn't matter anymore. The longing for change becomes so much bigger that the fear just makes you stronger." He seemed so confident and at ease. It was exactly how Morgan wanted to feel.

"A promissory note, huh?"

James shook her hand and thanked her for coming to his store. "I hope to see you again."

"Oh you will. I'm sure of it." Morgan took her bag of peace and moved on to her supply store.

When she returned home that night, spending a bit more than she probably should have, she opened each new item that she got. For one, she wanted a new mixing bowl. She wanted something that was a different color than she'd been using for so long. Something that would add some cheer to her kitchen. She wanted new muffin and cake pans, new measuring spoons and just to make her feel more peppy, a red apron. She took out the red apron and put it on. She started cleaning her new supplies and took out the flour and sugar she would need for her next batch of treats. She turned on a bit of music to just relax and it was at that very moment, her phone rang.

"It's Morgan." She answered with a touch of busyness in her voice.

"Any luck on the job hunt?"

"And hello to you too, mom. I'm doing well, how are you?"

"Morgan, you don't have much time to figure out what you're going to do. Make sure you get the letter of recommendation they offered. Remember to not burn bridges and keep good terms with everyone there. Right now, times are—"

"Mom? I'm not going to be looking for a job."

This time her mother simply held her silence.

"Mom?"

"I guess it's your life, Morgan. I just hope that one day, you will grow up and make something of it." She didn't say goodbye. She just ended the call.

It was a lonely night for Morgan and one that awakened a lot of self doubt, a lot of fear and as strange as it was to her, a lot of dreams she didn't even know she had. When the buzzer for her Apricot Cake went off, it briefly took her mind away from the negative and let her focus on the sweet. She pulled out her decorating bags and filled them with her homemade whipped cream and frosting and made a beautiful cake, perfect for a bridal shower. After appreciating the cake in its entirety, she knew it was time to delve into just one slice, a plentiful one at that. And so she did. She cut a stunningly layered piece of Apricot cake, drizzled with almond slices and coconut shavings. This time she patted her own back.

She had a small deck just outside her family room and never took advantage of her own small bistro set that she picked up at a local grocery mart sale. Tonight was a good night to enjoy the crisp cool air and watch the neighbors come home from their jobs. Just before heading outside she noticed a subscription to one of her many magazines she never read. On the cover was a headline that said, "Better, Faster, Different." Morgan emphatically replied, "Yes, please." With her plate in one hand, coffee cup in the other, she kneeled down with impressive skill and snatched the magazine with her mouth and headed to the deck. She slid open the cracked door with her foot and sat down on the padded bistro chair. She set her coffee down, along with the plated pastry and opened the magazine to the appropriate page. She took a bite as she sunk a little deeper into the chair and read.

Better, Faster and Different
By Harry Paul
Coauthor of *FISH! A Proven Way to boost Morale and Improve Results*

Lew Platt, former CEO of Hewlett Packard said, "Whatever made you successful in the past, won't in the future." Truer words were never spoken. Was it that long ago when we went to purchase a new cell phone the salesperson would ask us, "would you like to add the optional shoulder strap"? Now our cell phones are smaller than a deck of playing cards and as powerful as many laptop computers. To survive and thrive in today's world we must be BFD. Better, faster and different. If not, we'll end up like the proverbial buggy whip manufacturer. The opposite of innovation is insanity. Albert Einstein's definition of insanity is, "Doing the same thing over and over again and expecting different results."

We can't sit idly by and think that we don't need to innovate. Innovation is the number one export of the United States. Other countries may be better at manufacturing or processing—but they are working with our innovative ideas and designs. The United States exports brilliance. All you have to do is watch the ABC show "Shark Tank." Look at the new, creative and innovative ideas people are pitching to investors. When a challenge is put to us the sky's the limit, literally. When President John F. Kennedy challenged this country in the early sixties to send a man to the moon, land him and bring him back safely, by the end of the decade, wishing and hoping did not accomplish this— innovation did. And they did it without microchips and with computers using vacuum tubes. There wasn't even a hand-held digital calculator back then; they were using slide rules. Also, think of the innovation that went into the successful failure of Apollo 13 launched on April 11, 1970. NASA practically had to reinvent all their procedures to bring the astronauts home safely.

Look at where you are now and where you want to be in the future—what will get you there—innovation? We all need to constantly reinvent who we are and what we are doing. The first person I heard say, "You're either green and growing, or ripe and rotting" was Ray Kroc, founder of McDonald's, He started the firm in his 50's-- it's never too late to innovate. McDonald's is constantly innovating and yes they sell more hamburgers than anyone else, but they also sell more coffee than Starbucks.! They are always looking for new ways to do business.

There are a few things that we can do to keep innovating so it becomes a useful tool we can use to survive and thrive no matter who we are or what we are doing.

1.  Don't be afraid of change. Change happens. Embrace it and look at it as an opportunity to do things differently
2.  It's okay to let go of things familiar to you; ways you go to business; how you work with people; how you set goals

3. And when you see something you want to change make sure you use the three "Ds" of innovation"

## Disposition

Have a can-do attitude and a belief that we don't always have all the answers. We need to build an Army of Advocates who want us to and are willing to help us succeed. This will only occur with a winning attitude.

## Desire

Have passion and belief in what you are trying to accomplish. If you don't believe in it—it won't happen. I have this passion for the book *FISH!* that I coauthored. My passion is paramount because of my belief in the message, which fueled my burning desire to do what it takes in spreading the *FISH!* Philosophy. Now *FISH!* is one of the best selling business books of all time.

## Dedication

There will be distracters to your innovative ideas and concepts. One of my favorite quotes is by poet and author, Ella Wheeler Wilcox, "There is no chance, no destiny no fate, that can circumvent, hinder or control the firm resolve of a determined soul." Don't let anyone get you down and distract you from coming up with new ideas and concepts and putting them to work.

Start looking at what and how you are doing what it is you are doing and start looking at different ways of doing it. Keeping it fresh, full of energy, excitement and passion. Always take the approach, as I do, that there are no bad ideas, just ideas that are good for me and ideas that are better for someone else. That way you will look at opportunities with a fresh perspective, a can-do attitude and creativity leading to innovation. Innovation is good for you, your company and the United States of America. Keep it going!

Morgan barely made it to the second bite. Was he writing this just for her? How long was this magazine sitting with that stack before she would read it? How much more information was swimming around her apartment that she never bothered to take in? Sitting idly. That's exactly what she felt like for the past ten years at Superior Staffing, not to mention the prior twenty years trying to hold down boring job after boring job. She felt way too ripe and she wasn't nearly ready to rot. Now was the time for her to keep up and grow. But how? She was terrified of change and here she was forced to change this very moment. Maybe it wasn't so awful after all. But, did she have the passion and the dedication to see this change through? It was time to find out.

Her first mission? Promissory notes.

She licked the last bits of sweetness on her fingers and brought in her plate to the kitchen sink. She left the doors open to feel the cool breeze and hear the buzz of neighbors on the streets. She dimmed the lights to create a warm feeling within her and grabbed a stack of papers and one pen. Promissory note number one would begin with her mother. The next, her father. After that, her sister. She even wrote notes to Rachel at Superior Staffing. She wrote a note to Alicia and everyone that shared her floor. She wrote a note to her great aunt whom she only met once, but told her that anything she imagined could be a reality. She wrote a note to her boss from twenty years ago who had fired her for being too slow on the water refills. She searched her mind for everyone she knew who had even a glimpse of impact in her life. And lastly, she wrote a note to James, the man behind this whole idea and who sold her the most calming delicious tea. By the time she was finished she had over three-hundred promissory notes, all pledging her dream and humbly asking for support. She was pleasantly surprised that she knew that many people. And there would be more. She knew this.

The night went into the next day. By the time the letters were written and they were appropriately addressed, she was spent. The energy high was shifting into exhaustion.

But, it was the kind that sent her off into a deeper rest than she'd had in a long time.

*There comes a moment when you have to stop revving the car and shove it into gear.*

— David Maloney

*Chapter 3*

# LIFE APPLICATION
# BECOMING AN INITIATIVE NINJA

Feeling happy was proving to be key in Morgan's motivation. But, there was one thing that consistently killed that motivation. Morgan listened to the voicemail of the call she missed while in the shower.

"Morgan, it's your mother. I don't understand this note you sent me." Morgan could hear her mother scuffling the note on the message. "Anyhow, there's an opening for an assistant at Steve's accounting firm and they've put in a good word for you. You should jump on it." She hung up. There was no goodbye.

Morgan deleted the message and finished dressing. She combed her hair back out of her face and grabbed her now neatly organized purse and headed out the door. She tried hard to keep up the momentum, but as she thought about her money running out and her mom's persistent calls about getting another job, she couldn't help but lose the impetus she'd only just learned she had. Was this a set-back? She didn't quite understand. She thought having the initiative and thirst to do anything at all should be enough, but it wasn't. Apparently this would be something she'd have to work at.

In the middle of the busy street, she felt the urgent need to collapse onto the nearest bench. She let out a big, almost moan like sigh and let her purse fall to her side.

"Are you alright?" The woman spoke softly and seemed genuinely concerned.

Morgan, caught off guard, noticed that she'd dropped her purse on the woman's leg. "I'm so sorry," Morgan quickly retorted.

"No, no, it's fine. But, are you?"

"Oh, yes. I mean no. Well, I don't really know. I guess I just got a little light headed and I'm not even sure why." She laughed while displaying her discomfort.

"Looks like you might have caught something from someone else." The woman seemed quite sure.

"Oh, I don't know. I don't really feel ill or anything." Morgan wasn't sure why this woman cared so much.

"Stuff."

"Excuse me?" Morgan didn't understand and the anxiety felt so intense, the only she wanted to understand was how to get rid of it.

"You must have caught someone else's stuff. Just release it." The woman turned back to purse, where she pulled out some hand lotion. It was as if she never said anything to Morgan at all. But still, Morgan waited for more. The woman continued to sit quietly.

"I don't think I'm following you." Morgan finally pushed.

The woman turned toward Morgan. "Your name?"

"I'm Morgan."

"Morgan, I'm Deborah Clark and I've caught a lot of people's stuff. The stuff you don't want to catch. The negative responses to the things you do. Their fears and disbeliefs. Their depression and their insecurities. Fortunately, I've caught it all."

Morgan raised her eyes and questioned this woman's sanity for a brief moment. "Fortunately? That doesn't sound too fortunate to me."

"I caught it and then I released it. Each time it brought me into better focus of what I wanted."

Morgan nodded.

"You follow me now?" Deborah nodded back.

"Yeah, I think caught something from my mother a long time ago and I still haven't released it." She looked at Deborah with more curiosity. "Can I ask how someone releases that 'stuff'?"

"I was hoping you would." She smiled and turned her body towards Morgan. "I believe that we all choose the role we want to play. It's up to us whether we want to be a victim to what other people do or say to us. It's also up to us to release what they do and say and choose a different role."

"Wow. All along it was my choice?"

"Yep. And it always will be." She looked Morgan up and down. "Morgan, right?"

Morgan nodded.

"You have gifts Morgan. We all do. Do a life application on yourself and rediscover those gifts. Be grateful for them. Every time someone throws you something to catch. Catch it and then release. Let it remind you of where you want to go."

A car pulled up as Deborah finished her words. "That's my ride." She stood up and held her hand out. "It was a pleasure meeting you, Morgan."

Morgan stood up to return the handshake and noticed that she felt surprisingly better. "Thank you, Deborah. Really, thank you."

Deborah smiled and walked to the car that waited.

Morgan thought about the things her mother said to her while growing up. She thought about the way she praised her sister's career growth, while demoting her own. She accounted for all of the times that her parent's desires overpowered what she might have wanted for herself. It wasn't until getting fired from Superior Staffing that she ever put any attention on what she wanted. The ideas were snuffed out as soon as they were lit. But, was that her mother's fault? How could she blame someone else for the way she acted? Wasn't it time for her to take action?

She continued to walk along the city sidewalks until she came across a sports bar. Just outside on the patio were two young women enjoying an ice tea and lemonade. "Perfect," she thought. It was just what she needed.

She nodded to the bartender for a table. "Anywhere is fine," he returned with a smile. Morgan took a seat at one of the high tables and ordered lemonade. She turned her attention to hear the televisions that were not playing sports and instead showing an interview. The bar was quiet now and held only Morgan, the two women and an elderly gentleman.

"Talk is cheap," said the distinguished man on the screen. "How many times have we heard that discussion growing up?"

Morgan agreed in her mind and her smile reflected it.

The bartender brought her drink and asked if she'd like the volume turned up.

"Sure, I mean if no one else minds," she responded.

"I don't think so. Besides he's an interesting guy. Worth the listen."

"Thanks." She took a sip of the sweet and refreshing lemonade and continued to listen.

"Don't believe it. Talk can cost you everything." The man continued. He sat in a studio with an attractive correspondent just across from him. The camera switched back and forth between the two.

"Have you ever known someone who wasted his or her life's bank account, their character and reputation and self-esteem, by choosing to talk, but not take the actions that transform their ideas into reality?" He was very poised and to the point.

"Who is this guy?" Morgan asked the bartender.

"That's Gary Goldstein. He's a film producer and author," the bartender answered as he set prepared drinks on a tray.

"It's the little choices and small steps we take each day that add up to living our potential, expanding our capacity, enjoying a fulfilling and exciting life journey." Morgan was getting inspired by this man's words and couldn't turn herself from watching. "It's the intentional actions you take, the quality of thoughts you allow yourself to think, the success-minded people with whom you surround yourself, the way you practice your life each day that define over time a happy, rich, accomplished, satisfying life."

Morgan watched him speak with such influence. She questioned the people she surrounded herself with and what her daily practices had been up until this point. No wonder she felt unaccomplished and dissatisfied with her life.

"Initiative. A simple word, but it's the single quality and character trait that divides the doers from the dreamers." Initiative. There it was again. The trait she always lacked. And here he was, Gary Goldstein talking to millions of people and it felt as if he was talking just to her. "Do you believe you're meant to do something special in this precious human journey that is your life?" He looked into the camera as he spoke.

Morgan quietly answered, "Yes."

# Chapter 4

# THE GAIN OF LOSS
# NEVER MET A STRANGER

As the days went on and the two-week severance was running out, Morgan realized how much she despised feeling uncomfortable. Change was quite uncomfortable. So much so that she questioned whether she should call her mother back and interview for the job. At least then she would have a paycheck coming in and something she had to be accountable. There she went again, reverting back to the same thoughts that kept her at a standstill for so long. "Maybe the search for fulfillment doesn't always make you feel so fulfilled," she thought as she cleaned her bathroom. For a moment, she paused and watched herself in the mirror. She looked into her own eyes and there it was. Fear. It was written all over her face. She was being pushed now by no one but herself and it was quite possibly the scariest feeling she'd had since going on a first date. A first date had been so long ago she didn't even remember whether she was a brunette like now or going through her blonde stage at the time. She shook her head at her reflection. Tears filled her eyes as the worries came pouring in. What was she going to do? How could she turn new wisdom she was given into a future?

When she came out of the bathroom she looked at the clock. "Dammit!" She was going to be late. She nearly forgot that she had a lunch planned with Jayne and Peter Stanyon. Jayne and Peter were the parents of her best friend in high school. Her best friend Kirsty and sister Hollie had passed away in a car accident and she forever remained close with Jayne and Peter. They were the kindest people Morgan had ever known. In fact, she wished her parents were more like them. She remembered her mother always apologizing to them for their loss. But, they always seemed confused by the notion. To them, there was no loss. There was only a gain. Morgan never quite understood whether they had actually grieved or not. She never really knew what they meant. All she knew was the feeling of loss she experienced. Today, she would ask them.

Sitting outside the Italian restaurant overlooking the ocean, Morgan realized that Jayne and Peter were probably one of the few dates she ever kept her commitment. "Such a beautiful day," Jayne admired.

"Yes, it is." Morgan agreed.

"So, tell us, Morgan, what's been going on with you? What's new and exciting?" Jayne was so uplifting. Morgan loved being around her. She was always well-dressed and her face so bright.

"Well, I don't have a job now. I got fired and I'm in the most frightening transition period of my life."

"Ah! Congratulations!" Peter joined in.

"Huh?"

"Yes, good for you, Morgan!" Jayne added.

Morgan looked at them both. She was never shocked at their reactions, but only shocked that it took her so long to find out why they reacted in the complete opposite of textbook standard ways to react to tragedy. "Ok. Jayne? Peter? I have to ask…" Jayne and Peter waited with smiles. "Whenever something goes wrong, you don't get upset. How is that?"

"Well, it's not that we don't get upset." Jayne answered. "It's more about how we choose to live our life. We feel it for a short time then we let it go and embrace the new."

"Pardon me for saying so, but…," Morgan lowered her voice so as not to insult them. "Well, it just doesn't seem normal."

"And what's that?" Jayne asked.

Morgan thought for a minute. "Um, well I guess it would be normal to sulk when things go wrong."

"Yeah, you know, we've done that. And I have to say, it's quite miserable, life's way too short to be unhappy."

Morgan laughed at her bluntness. "I guess you're right."

"You know, Morgan, there's a typical way that people expect you should respond to tragedy or to hardships, but that doesn't mean it's what you should do."

Morgan continued to listen.

"Our world could have ended by the tragic loss of our daughters, but instead we grieved and felt the sadness for a time and then we shifted our thoughts."

"How do you mean?" Morgan asked.

"It feels so good to remember all the great things Kirsty and Hollie gave to us, the precious memories we have are priceless. Our girls have taught us many life lessons and it's because of them that we've shifted our entire lives. In a sense, the tragedy brought new light to our lives and we are in a state of gratitude now for what Kirsty and Hollie have given us rather than a state of loss for what was taken away." Jayne spoke with such appreciation.

Morgan couldn't help but smile with her. "I never would have thought about it that way. You know all these years, I found myself wanting to be just like you two. I wanted to know your secrets to enjoying life despite the loss you've had. I just never had the courage to ask how or why."

"Well, we're glad you did," Peter said.

"You're in an exciting position now, Morgan," Jane continued. "Don't look at this as the end of something. Look at it as a new beginning. An opportunity for something bigger and better. You are in a frightening transition, yes.

But, look at the good and focus on how exciting it is. You can do whatever you want."

Morgan could feel something different pumping through her veins as she listened to Jane speak. She knew that if she and Peter could shift their lives and see the gain of loss, then so she could shift also.

As Morgan walked home after meeting with Jayne and Peter, she saw her favorite café and walked in again for little dessert to cap off the delicious angel hair pasta she had for lunch. It was busy this time in the afternoon, but she didn't mind waiting in line. In front of her was a young man, chatting away with an older man waiting ahead of him. They laughed a lot and it made Morgan smile. They seemed to be long time friends.

"Alright Kent, it's been great. I'll see you soon," the older man said to the younger man standing in front of Morgan. He walked off with his coffee drink and bag of goodies.

"Yeah, man. I'll see you around!" The young man, Kent, noticed Morgan watching them and smiled back to her. "How are you doing today?" It was as if he'd seen her before.

Truthfully, Morgan felt great. She hadn't felt better in a long time. It was a vast difference than she felt that morning. "I'm great. You two seem to be great friends, you must have known each other a long time."

Kent turned to the barista behind the counter and placed his order and then went back to Morgan. "No, actually we just met."

"Really?"

"Yeah." He paid the lady at the counter and then said to Morgan. "I've never met a stranger."

"How is that possible?"

"I realized something when my mother passed away." Morgan waited for him to continue. "If you treat everyone you meet like they're family, you change everything. "

Morgan nodded, trying to soak that in.

"It's about the people you know and the connections you make."

"Instead of what you know?"

"You got it." He smirked a cute smile. "I'm Kent Georgi by the way. I'll see you around..." He tilted his head in question, prompting her to fill in the blank.

"Morgan! I'm Morgan."

"Right. I'll see you around, Morgan."

"You bet, Kent!" He gave her a thumbs up for catching his name and then waved goodbye as he got his order.

Morgan turned towards the barista and read her name tag. With a smile, she said, "Hi, Molly. Beautiful today, isn't it?"

*Chapter 5*

# BRIGHTEN UP
# SIMPLY DO WHAT YOU NEED TO DO
# KNOCK AND IT SHALL BE OPENED
# WAIT FOR THE REVEAL
# RE-KNEW

It had been a week now and there was one more week of survival money left. Well, technically she had a small amount in savings, but the lot of it was being expended on a sinfully thrilling addiction to bake ware. Morgan was practically making daily visits to Café la Claire and Stanley's Cake and Bake Supply Store just after. She never had the time before or made the time to walk along the local streets of the neighborhood she said she wanted to live in. After all of these years, she was finally enjoying the quirky shops and entrancing people watching. Her mind was opening more and her thoughts were evolving. Everything was changing, but she didn't know whether it was good or not. She felt better when she went to the café and she felt more vibrant after leaving Stanley's. Even if she only walked through the store without buying a thing, she felt inspired. It was a feeling she hadn't experienced before and if she had, the time lapse between now and then made it unrecognizable. This was definitely new. She felt as if the doors to the world she saw everyone else playing around in were cracking open for her to get a glimpse. She just needed to figure out how to open those doors all the way. Amongst all of these new bright and exciting feelings, there was still the fear. The "what ifs" kept climbing their way to the surface and the more she would try to fight them, the more present they made themselves.

It was usually about this time in the morning that the anxiety would rise and also about the time that she knew she must leave for her walk. It was the only thing that pushed her closer to the world she wanted to be in.

"Morgan, right?" Molly, the young girl behind the counter asked as she handed Morgan her quiche and coffee.

"Yep." Morgan responded cheerfully as her mouth began salivating from the aromas.

"This is for you." She handed Morgan a purple folded paper with her name on it.

"A woman named Donna told me to give this to you." Morgan grabbed it with enthusiasm and remembered Donna right away. "It's a good thing you introduced yourself the other day or I would have no clue who Donna wanted to have this."

"Wow, thank you so much." Morgan took the paper and her snack and gave a silent thanks to Kent for giving her the courage to say hi to Molly that day.

When she opened the paper, she noticed a note at the top. "What to do when no one is looking." She looked below and it was a baking class that was to begin that very night. "Lighten Up: With Icing on the Top!" was the name of the class. Morgan took a bite of her quiche and closed her eyes as it made its warm way to her stomach. She licked the pesto on her fingers and then read, "Raspberry filled cakes and edible pearls, fondant masterpieces and chocolate swirls, it's a class guaranteed to satisfy your soul and in this class, I let you lick right out of the bowl!" She read on for the time, place and number to call. A shot of adrenaline rushed through her body. She could feel it in her heart and right to the stomach. She took out her phone and started to dial, but ended the call after a total of three failed attempts. She read Donna's note again at the top and she reflected on the past few days. She wrote those notes to everyone she knew and now was the time to take action and follow through with those promises. She dialed the number.

"Hi, this is Rhonda." Her voice painted a picture of a sunflower.

"Oh, hi. Um, I'm calling about the class tonight with Raelyn."

"Fabulous! Raelyn is a very good friend of mine. She's an amazing pastry chef and artist and as sweet as can be. I've organized this class for her. You are sure to meet some fantastic people. It starts at seven and we'll go till nine. Address is on the flyer." She was quick, but caring.

"Great."

"What's your name, hun?"

"I'm Morgan."

"Great Morgan, we'll see you then. Feel free to bring any of your favorites, however we'll have everything you need there. All you need is some color."

"Ok." But, before she hung up, she said, "Wait, color? What do you mean by that?"

"Oh" She laughed cheerfully. "Well, the purpose of the class is to bring color to our lives. So, we ask that the students wear their best clothes with the brightest colors. You just bake better!"

"Really?" Morgan was very confused now as to what type of class she was taking."I'll bake better if I'm dressed in color?"

"Try it. You'll see. We all have a heavy load at one time or another. You operate best when you can lighten it up. When you wear your best, you feel your best."

"Ok, I guess I'll try it then." Morgan figured she had nothing to lose. The question was where she could find something bright that made her feel good. She remembered that one of the dress shops near her favorite café was having a sale.

The racks outside displayed beautiful dresses, but nothing that grabbed Morgan. When she turned around to look at another rack, she accidentally bumped into someone else. "Oh, excuse me! I'm so sorry."

"Oh! No problem!" The petite blonde seemed to welcome the bump.

"I'm so focused on finding something with color," Morgan laughed nervously questioning why she was giving this woman an excuse.

"Really? What for?" The woman seemed very interested.

Surprised, Morgan answered, "I'm taking this class and they suggested that I wear something with color to brighten up I guess."

"Hmm, I can see what they mean."

"You can? Because I'm sort of confused."

"Color can actually shift your emotional energy."

"Really?"

"Oh, absolutely!" The woman reached inside her purse and pulled out a card. "Here."

Morgan looked at the card and discovered that this woman, Dr. Martha Reed was actually an expert in the field of empowering minds through the use of color. "Ok, wow. I couldn't have run into a more suitable person."

Martha nodded at the irony. "Hey, I have an idea."

"Ok," Morgan agreed.

Martha scanned the inside of the store until her eyes rested on something. "Come over here."

Morgan followed.

Martha picked up two scarves that were folded on display. She ruffled them out. One was dark blue and the other was a bright sky blue. She held up the dark blue against Morgan and led her to a mirror. "What's your first response? How do you feel?"

Morgan looked at herself with the dark navy blue and focused her attention on the color. "Well, I feel warm. I feel cozy. It makes me feel relaxed, like I should be drinking hot chocolate on a rainy day by the fire."

Martha smiled, "Ok, good." She took the dark blue away and then held up the light blue. "And this?"

Morgan immediately lifted her head up and smiled. "Energy. I feel more energy with this one. I feel like I want to go take a brisk walk along the water. I feel… inspired."

Martha put both of the scarves down. "Did you feel the internal shift of energy and emotion with the use of different colors?"

"That was amazing!" Morgan said. "And so simple."

"Well, it's something I use with my clients for all reasons."

"Thank you…" Morgan looked down at the card again.

"Just call me Martha."

When she walked up to the double steel doors just outside the one-story building, she noticed a group of students already waiting. Some had aprons hanging from their arms, some had bake ware with them and some had nothing but the purple flyer and scared looks on their faces. Everyone waited.

"Those doors won't open themselves." A man walking up asserted.

Everyone turned to look at him, including Morgan. He was wearing a bright blue shirt. In fact, as Morgan looked around, everyone had followed instructions quite well in dressing with color. Everyone, but her. She looked down at her pale grey dress that took her at least an hour to decide on. The truth was, nothing in her closet boasted color and now more than ever she understood the effect it could have.

The man opened the door and headed in. To everyone's surprise the door was indeed open and the teacher was already inside setting up.

The man in the blue shirt had a certain confidence about him that caught Morgan's attention.

"Hi everyone, my name is Raelyn. Please take a spot behind any counter space you can find. In a short moment my friend Lane Ethridge will be speaking to you all." She was sweet in her introduction. "I like to start my classes off right and he spreads a powerful message that means a lot to me and I'd love to share it with all of you before we begin!"

Everyone shuffled to get a good spot. Morgan walked around and noticed one woman who still had an empty spot next to her and set her purse down and smiled.

"Hi everyone! I'm Lane and I'm here to support my good friend Raelyn and to hopefully inspire you all to make the best pastries you, and whoever tries them, have ever tasted. Whether you are here to try something new or indulge in a passion, I hope that you will all remember to believe in what it is that you ultimately want. One of my favorite quotes from my favorite book affirms that when you 'Ask and it shall be given to you; seek and ye shall find; knock and it shall be opened to you.' It's my hope that you are all here because you are fulfilling a desire. If you find yourself unfulfilled, why are you, with your skills and talents, not where you want to be?" He looked at each person and held a few moments on Morgan. "I wish you all to shine in this class as it will cause you all to shine. Enjoy your class!"

The class thanked Lane and Raelyn for bringing him. Morgan smiled and finished setting up her area.

"Do you bake often?" The woman next to Morgan asked her.

"Actually, I do. I mean when I can. I love it. It makes me feel…just good I guess." The woman smiled and nodded. "How about you?" Morgan asked.

"Well, I've never taken it seriously. This was actually a gift from a friend, but I'll tell you what, I'm excited!" She tied her long brown wavy hair back with a rubber band and then reached for an apron. "Oh, I'm Rosemary Medel by the way." Once her hand was free she held it out.

Morgan finished tying on her own apron and welcomed the handshake. "I'm Morgan." She looked around the classroom and noticed the variety of students. "Yeah, I'm excited too."

Rosemary was very warm with a distinct sense of confidence. She took notice of Morgan's less than comfortable stance in the class. "So, what brought you here Morgan?"

Morgan appreciated that Rosemary was taking interest. "Well, this woman, um a friend I guess." She smiled thinking about Donna. "She told me about it. I guess she figured that I love baking."

"Hmm." It seemed Rosemary wasn't thrilled with her answer, but would let it go. She started to rearrange her baking area.

Morgan on the other hand didn't want to let it go. "I lost my job." Morgan retorted.

Rosemary nodded as if she knew there was something else.

"I'm trying to figure out what to do and yet all I can do is think about making pastries." She laughed out loud at how absurd it sounded when she actually spoke the words. She felt old and ridiculous. She figured most of the people in that room were there for the simple joy of baking and probably had successful careers and lives at home. Here she was in her forties trying to figure it all out.

"So what's your plan?" Rosemary asked.

Morgan froze for a few beats. "Well, that's the thing. I don't really have one."

"Create your plan B." Rosemary was direct with her response as if it was an obvious next step.

"What?" It sounded so simple, but as with most things, Morgan complicated the simple. It just seemed easier that way.

"When plan A doesn't work out, go to plan B." Rosemary was matter of fact about it.

"I have no idea what Plan B is." Morgan could feel the instantaneous pressure and guilt of not having a Plan B.

"So make one."

"But, where do I begin?"

Rosemary circled her head throughout the room. "Look around you. There's opportunity everywhere. Your friend sent you here and you accepted it."

"I almost didn't."

"But, you did." She gave Morgan a reassuring look. "You're investing in yourself."

Morgan didn't think of that way, but just as soon as Rosemary said it, she felt at ease. "I was so nervous to come, but I'm so tired of being nervous and scared about everything, you know?"

"Oh, yes. Believe me. I know."

"Really?" Morgan was surprised that this woman ever experienced a day of fear in her life.

"There was a time when every change in life freaked me out. I couldn't understand why things wouldn't go according to my first plan. It frustrated me to the point of wanting to give up. But, that didn't get me anywhere."

Morgan felt the connection to Rosemary right away. "What did you do?"

"Learned to be flexible and do what I needed to do."

"But, how did you know what that was?"

Rosemary related to Morgan and turned towards her at that moment. "Risk is scary. I know that. Losing a job and having to start all over. It's a risk. You've got to get out there and do something else. But, there's opportunity in every risk you take. Be flexible and you'll feel much more at ease with every step you take. Don't get tied to one outcome. If one plan doesn't work, move on to the next. Everyone experiences a change in course. It's going to happen no matter what. Accepting it and being flexible to the changes that come will only make it a better ride. Just because something ends and doesn't turn out the way you want, doesn't mean it's the end. It's just the beginning of something else." She paused for a moment to study Morgan who was hanging on to every word. "You're in an exciting position Morgan. You get to do what you need to do, that's it."

Morgan nodded as she infused herself with this new notion. "I think I get it. But, how do I start? How do I let go of feeling like a failure?"

"You have a lot of courage Morgan and maybe you don't see it yet, but you do. Use that same courage to evaluate yourself. Look inside and recognize what you're scared of and have the nerve to get what you really really want." She looked around the room. "I have a feeling you know what that is."

Morgan smiled because she did know. "Thank you."

"Let's get baking shall we?"

The class would end in about one half hour and Morgan was riding high like never before. Her *choux* pastry dough was just about done and ready to pull out of the oven. She hopped over to the sink to wash her hands from cleaning her area and then pranced right back over to the oven to peek. When she turned on the light she crinkled her face and sighed. "Ugh."

"Just wait." A man from behind her said.

Only seeing his shoes, she spoke back to him. "No, I've done this enough to know that they aren't as perfect as I'd hoped." She shook her head feeling the deflation of high take over. She stood up and drew her eyes to the height of the man standing behind her. He was tall. Very tall. "Were you here the whole time?"

He laughed. "You would have remembered."

"Yes! I would have."

"No, I'm picking up a friend who needed a ride. That and I can't deny freshly baked dessert." He had a great laugh. It was almost addictive and it made Morgan smile.

"You didn't strike me as a baker," Morgan agreed.

"Oh yeah? Why not?"

"You aren't, are you?"

"I might be. What makes you think I'm not?"

Morgan looked him up and down. "Well, you just seem very masculine and like you'd rather be out on the road doing guy stuff rather than licking icing off of your fingers."

"And that's why there's so many missed opportunities in life," he quickly added.

"Missed opportunities?"

"It's easy to make an assumption about someone based on looking at them. Sometimes you might be right. But, you never quite know until you get to know them."

"Hmm. I guess so. But, what about first impressions?" Morgan asked him.

"A first impression is just a first impression. Unfortunately people make a lot of decisions based on that first impression and don't allow the person to reveal themselves. Then they miss out on someone or something really great."

"Randy! We'll be done in about fifteen. Can you hang around?" Raelyn called out to him.

"You got it," Randy answered.

"Oh, you're Raelyn's friend?"

"Yep. Randy Hausauer." He smiled.

"Well, you've given me good food for thought."

"Don't be so quick to judge on that dough in there. Give it a chance. Pull it out. Taste it. It might be the best damn dough you ever made, regardless of what it looks like."

Morgan gave Randy a great big grin and then turned her attention to the head of the class to hear Raelyn. "It's about that time everyone. Let's pull out the dough and let it cool. Those who chose the *profiteroles* can meet me at station one. Those who chose to make the *religieuses*, I will meet you in five at station two."

Morgan watched Randy as he took a seat in the back to watch everyone. Despite looking so big and tough to Morgan, what stood out the most was his kindheartedness. She turned to her assigned oven and pulled out her less than perfect looking dough and tasted a tiny part. Delicious!

People grabbed their things and left the class. Morgan noticed all of them a bit looser than they began. She vowed to herself to wear pink at the next class.

The class wasn't far from home and she enjoyed the crisp temperate air as she strolled along the closed shops and full trees. The night was quiet and the only sound filling the air was her flip flops smacking against her heels with each step and the sounds of fading voices as she walked further from the culinary school. She held her tray of *religieuses* and couldn't wait to get home, sit on her couch, make tea and indulge.

Smash! "Ugh!" She heard the sound of something fall and break just behind her and turned to look.

"Are you okay?"

"Yeah, I was just enjoying my walk so much that I forgot to look down at the pothole!" His name was Randy and he was another student in class.

"I didn't even hear you behind me." She said as she helped him pick up the fallen items.

"I bet you did now." He laughed.

"You're the other Randy, right?" she asked.

"Yep, Randy Ngan," he said.

"On your way home?" she questioned.

"Yeah, I live two blocks from here."

"Funny. Me, too. So how'd you like the class?"

"Well, it's one of Raelyn's first classes at that school and she and I went to school together way back when. She's a close friend and I think she was a little nervous that not enough people would show up. But, I liked it. Definitely something different. You seemed to really enjoy it, though."

"You could tell?"

"I can tell when someone likes to learn."

"I think I'm just realizing that it's the something I've always wanted to do," Morgan admitted to herself and to him.

"That's awesome! So, what are you going to do about it?" He didn't hold back.

Morgan was taken aback, but it forced her to think. "Well, I guess I'm just now trying to figure that out."

"Want to know an easy way to figure it out?"

"Are you kidding me? Yes! Please divulge it to me!" They both laughed.

"Ask yourself if what you want is possible."

"Ok."

"Then see if it's attainable for you."

"I say yes to both," she exclaimed, excited that she felt that way at all.

"You're half way there."

"Then what?" She was as eager as she felt in a long time.

"Find someone who's already done it and follow the path."

"That's it?" She squinted at him with disbelief.

"That's it. Don't make it hard. It is that simple. Try it. You'll see, the rest will come as it should."

She stopped in the middle of the sidewalk and took it all in. "Wow, I feel…"

"Renewed?"

"Kind of, yeah." She thought about it some more. "Yes, actually. Renewed. I do. I feel renewed. It's like the simpler it is the more clear it is."

"Whenever I want to accomplish something I always go back to those four steps. I call it my re-knewal process.

Stop making things so difficult. Just ask those who have done it."

"You know Randy, I just got fired from my job and I keep thinking that I'm supposed to feel really bad about it, but I'm finding more times that I'm not, I'm getting excited about it."

Randy smiled. "Well, I'm right up this street. Will I see you at the next class?"

"You bet!" She continued to walk along feeling every ounce of appreciation for the people she met and especially for Donna who had persuaded her to grab this opportunity.

# Chapter 6

# SUPPORT CELL
# SUCCESS IN TWO
# THE POWER OF INITIATIVE

It was almost impossible to fall asleep the first hour she was lying in bed. But, apparently she had. The next thing she knew was being awakened by the sound of garbage truck reversing in the alley of her apartment. It was all right with her, though. She jumped out of bed, rushed to the bathroom and looked in the mirror. She felt different and so she knew she must look different too.

"Looking good, Miss Morgan," she said to her reflection. "All you need is a little color and a bakery owner." She felt good about her mission for the day. She felt so good that her mother's latest phone call didn't faze her in the least.

After a leftover pastry for breakfast, she threw on some clothes and headed out. Her first stop would be the local thrift shop for bright colored clothes and maybe even a hat.

On her way out she saw Randy again. "You know we've probably walked by each other more times than we can count," she yelled out just behind him.

He turned around. "Oh, we have." He was about to continue walking on and then turned back to her. "You know, I came across someone the other day that might be of help to you."

"Really?" She was anxious to hear. "You've already been such a big help, I'm in!"

"His name is John and I think he could steer you in the right direction of getting where you need to go. Here." He reached into his pocket and grabbed his wallet. He fumbled through, found the card and handed it to Morgan. "Tell him Randy sent you."

"I will. Thank you so much."

"You got it. See you soon."


This whole idea of receiving advice and asking for help was new to Morgan. Awkwardly, unnervingly and painfully new. It was peculiarly awe-inspiring at the same time. She was starting to get the impression that it was, if truth be told, perfectly all right to ask for help. In fact, it wasn't long ago she met someone who told her that very concept. Funny, how she could actually hear what he said now.

Michael Hill was a family friend through her sister. She met him at a function they were having celebrating her sister's promotion to partner at the law firm she was working at.

"They call me Boot," he told Morgan at the buffet after she'd just been introduced by Maggie, her ever intelligent, beautiful and highly-successful younger sister.

"Why is that?" Morgan asked as she filled her plate with every mini torte and cake that filled the three-tiered dessert trays.

Maggie looked at Morgan's plate with her strikingly blue eyes and gestured to the other guests. "I'll leave you two to chat. I better get back to the guests."

"All right," Morgan blindly responded. She took one last chocolate cup filled with mousse and looked back to Boot. He had this great voice and easy way about him. She wanted to know more. "Boot?"

"I was a fighter pilot. That's what they called me." She could hear a hint of a drawl in his speaking and it made her smile inside.

"Wow. A fighter pilot? Really? Tell me more!" Morgan was excited. Her day-to-day activities included placing secretarial jobs and data entry jobs. Occasionally she got to place medical technicians at plastic surgery centers, but that was the extent of her interest being held.

"I wrote a book that could give you a good idea."

"Oh my goodness! I can't wait! What's it called?"

"Gravity." She could see the pride in his face as he said it.

"How'd you become a fighter pilot? If you don't mind me asking?" Morgan couldn't get enough of this guy who wasn't only interesting, but seemed as equally interested in everything around him.

He laughed right away. "Ha! That wasn't easy. Took me four years of getting rejected before they finally let me in."

"Four years of rejection? Why'd you stick around?" Her nose did its endearing crinkle that it always does when reacting to something that didn't seem so fair.

"That's just it. I stuck around. I kept going back and kept reapplying." He moved a little closer to Morgan and held his hand out as if carrying something. "It's like a tree. The fruit keeps getting lower and lower and the more you come back, the more likely you're going to get it."

Morgan shook her head in wonder. "I just don't know that I would have the same perseverance."

He stood back again. "Well you gotta have your support cell."

"Support cell?"

"Term we use in the air. You gotta have your 'go-to' people that support you and that thing you know you gotta to do." He thought for a minute, searching for another way to describe it. "It's like a mastermind group."

"Oh, like a group of people to bounce ideas off of?"

"That's it. You all help each other."

Morgan squinted and rummaged her memory for a saved contact list. "Uh. I think that would just be me."

"So, be your own support cell. Nothing wrong with that. Soon enough when you find that thing you gotta do 'cause it's the only thing that makes you tick, you'll find more. That's just the way it goes."

At the time, Morgan had no relationship with her dreams. They were as good as strangers. She could barely recognize what they might be even if she did see them once in a while. But, today, she knew. In fact, in just the past week, she probably formed more people that she could add to her support cell than she could in her lifetime thus far.

She deemed herself a regular at Café La Claire now, even if it hasn't been that long. It was part of her routine and for some reason it motivated her. She took her phone out as she waited for her croissant sandwich and held John Carmona's card in her hand. "Success in Two," she read aloud to herself. She dialed the number and listened to the ringing.

She heard the ending of a conversation in the background and then a clear, "This is John." He sounded uplifting.

"Hi, John. My name is Morgan. A friend referred me to you. His name is Randy?" She waited for the recognition. "Randy... I'm sorry I don't think I ever caught his last name."

"Some friend you are!" He joked with her. "Randy Ngan, yes."

"Yeah!" She felt elevated right away.

"What can I do for you?"

"You know, I'm not quite sure yet. But, he recommended I call you. I'm sort of in a transitional position right now."

"That's great!"

Another one, she thought. Everyone is so excited about her transitional phase. If only her mother could share in the excitement. "Apparently." She chuckled. "And so, well I guess I am calling for some guidance."

"I would love to serve you the best way I can."

"Your card says, Success in Two."

"That's right. I believe that no matter where you are, you can have success in just two years." He paused and then continued. "Now that isn't to say you won't experience success along the way. But, in my experience I've been able to bring any company or person to his or her ideal level of success within those two years."

"How do you figure two?" Morgan shifted her phone from one ear to the other and nodded to the waitress that brought her savory lunch and iced tea.

"It's a three step process. The first takes about six months."

"What happens in the six months?" she asked with her mouth full. "Sorry, I get excited when I learn something new and I eat when I get excited." She heard him laugh on the other end.

"Don't apologize. You should always take action on yourself and do what you love. If eating is it, then so be it!" She giggled in return and he went on, "Most people start something they really don't know that much about. Maybe they think they do, but there's usually a whole bunch of nuggets that they really need as they begin their new venture. In my history of clients, it's those first six months of being proactive and getting things in motion, where they really begin to understand what it is they are launching."

"Interesting. That makes complete sense." She could see in just this short period of time that she had already learned so much and still had room for so much more.

"The last six months of the first year is when you really understand what it is you need to do. You start to apply those things into the next year and it's those last six months of the second year where you see the results and you're profitable on every level."

Morgan was a little bit floored. It got her thinking. Could this really happen? Could she actually create a business out of doing something she loved? She still hadn't yet told anyone what it was that she wanted to do, but she knew that it was time to let it out and put it into action. There was no reason to keep it inside. Now, if any, was the best time for her to, "Open a bakery of my own," she blurted out from nowhere.

"Excuse me?" John was just finishing another sentence on the other end of the phone.

"I'm sorry. I didn't mean to interrupt. It's just that I haven't even told anyone. I think other people that I've only just met knew it even before I did. But, that's it."

"That's what?" John was a little confused now.

Morgan started laughing. "I must sound like a crazy person!"

John joined in on the laughs. "No, you actually sound like someone who's ready to get things rolling. But, what it is it again that you want to do?"

"I want my own bakery. I want to make the most delicious personalized cakes that make people smile. And . . . I'm really good at it, actually."

"Well, you got your first customer right here."

"Really?" Her heart was racing so much it was audible in her voice. "I know it might sound cheeky to some and my mother always told me it was a silly little girl dream, but I want to do it. Yeah. Yeah, that's what I want to do!" She looked around the café that she sat and realized that she was getting some looks, but she didn't care. She just entered their world and soon they would all be buying coconut cream pies and Shirley Temple themed cupcakes and *éclairs*. The best *éclairs* they'd ever have. "Success in two, John? You think?"

"I have no doubts. You're on your way."

She grinned so big, her eyes welled as she hung up the phone and soaked in the moment. The moment when she felt initiated into the world of those who have a plan; those who are resourceful, those who have the courage, the want and the drive to get what they want, she had it. She had that feeling right now and it was in full force.

As the sun went down, she tidied her home and sat on the couch to think for a moment. This was it. She was actually going to do it. But, how? Suddenly those doubts and fears came rippling back into her thoughts. And almost as if she were set to a telepathic timer, Morgan's mother called.

She tried to avoid the calls as often as she could, but she also knew that too much avoidance would lead to a bigger problem, so she just played busy when she did call. For some reason, she was keen to answer tonight, in the faint hopes of hopes, that her mother might share her exhilaration.

"Hi mom!" She purposely heightened the thrill in her voice.

"You got a job?" Her mother's smile was heard through the phone.

"Um, no."

Just as quickly as she heard the 'no', she said, "Oh."

"But, the good news is that I've started a baking class and I'm going to open a bakery. I'm creating a support cell and I'm going to fulfill the success that I promised to everyone I wrote my promissory notes to."

"Morgan, what are you talking about? Have you completely lost your mind?"

"Yes, mom. I think I have. Or I'm at least in the process of losing it and it feels really good. Scary, but good." There was a long break on the other end. "Mom?"

"Morgan, I really think you, me and your father should sit down and make a plan. You're just too . . . "

"Too what, mom?"

"You're just too old to be going through this dreamer like stage." With all efforts to be soft and compassionate, her mother said, "I think it's time you come up with a good plan and dad I will help you."

"Do you really want to help me, mom?"

"Well, of course, we do."

"Support me, mom. Both of you. Please, just support me in what I want to do. That's all I need."

"But, how will make your rent, how are you going to . . . ."

"I'll figure it out, mom. Remember? I'm old. I can do this."

"Morgan, I didn't mean—"

"It's okay, mom. You know what I need. Goodbye."

As soon as she hung up the phone she felt a huge release within her whole body. She felt lighter. So much so that she had to lie down.

But, going to bed that night proved to be just as much of a challenge as the last with all the thoughts of the day swarming around in her mind. She seemed to be experiencing every kind of emotion at once and though it was overwhelming, itdid not wearing her out enough to sleep just yet.

When her eyes finally gave into the heaviness, she heard her phone beep. She rolled over to turn off the sound and figured she would check it while she was at it. Maybe her mother would apologize and offer what she really wanted all this time. But, instead it was a text message from John.

"Check your email," it said. There was a smiley face just next to it.

From her phone she opened her email account and deleted a bunch of spam emails, ignored the job listings her mother sent her and went straight to John's email. The subject line said, "Found this just for you – someone you should learn from."

She opened the email, sat up with the first sentence and read.

The Power of Initiative
By: Brian Tracy

The world seems to belong to those who reach out and grab it with both hands. It belongs to those who do something rather than just wish and hope and plan and pray, and intend to do something someday, when everything is just right.

Successful people are not necessarily those who make the right decisions all the time. No one can do that, no matter how smart he is. But once successful people have made a decision, they begin moving toward their objectives step-by-step, and they begin to get feedback or signals to tell them where they're off course and when course corrections are necessary. As they take action and move toward their goals, they continually get new information that enables them to adjust their plans in large and small ways.

It's important to understand that life is a series of approximations and course adjustments. Let me explain. When an airplane leaves Chicago for Los Angeles, it is off course 99 percent of the time. This is normal and natural and to be expected. The pilot makes continual course corrections, a little to the north, a little to the south. The pilot continually adjusts altitude and throttle. And sure enough, several hours later, the plane touches down at exactly the time predicted when it first became airborne upon leaving Chicago. The entire journey has been a process of approximations and course adjustments.

What's the big problem? The big problem is that there are no guarantees in life. Everything you do—even crossing the street—is filled with uncertainty. You can never be completely sure that any action or behavior is going to bring about the desired result. There is always a risk. And where there is risk, there is fear. And whatever you think about grows in your mind and heart. People who think continually about the risks involved in any undertaking soon become preoccupied with fears and doubts and anxieties that conspire to hold them back from trying in the first place.

At Babson College, in a 12-year study into the reasons for success, researchers concluded that virtually all success was based on what they called the "corridor principle." They likened achieving success to proceeding down a corridor in life. Each of us stands at the entrance to this corridor, looking into the darkness, and we see the corridor disappear into the distance. The researchers said that the difference between the successes and the failures in their study could be summarized by the one word: launch! Successful people were willing to launch themselves down the corridor of opportunity without any guarantee of what would occur. They were willing to risk uncertainty and overcome the normal fears and doubts that hold the great majority in place.

And the remarkable thing is that as you move down the corridor of life, new doors of opportunity open up on both sides of you. However, you would not have seen those doors if you were not in the corridor, moving down the corridor. They would not have opened up for you if you had waited for some assurance before stepping out in faith and taking action.

The Confucian saying "A journey of a thousand leagues begins with a single step" simply means that great accomplishments begin with your willingness to face the inevitable uncertainty of any new enterprise and step out boldly in the direction of your goal.

Not long ago, a couple came to me with a problem. He was working for a company owned by his family in which he was bitterly unhappy. It was full of politics and backbiting and negativity, and he was stressed out and hated his job. He wanted to do something else but had no job offers or potential alternatives to his current position. He asked me for my advice on what to do.

I explained to him that there is a "vacuum principle of prosperity," which says that when you create a vacuum of any kind, nature rushes to fill it. In his case, this meant that as long as he stayed at his current job, there was no way that he could recognize other possibilities, and there was no way that other opportunities could find him. I told him to take a giant leap of faith and just walk away from his current job with no lifeline or safety net. I assured him that if he did, all kinds of things would open up for him that he simply couldn't see while he was locked up in his current situation.

He took my advice. He quit his job. The members of his family became very angry and told him that he would be unemployable outside of their business. But he stuck to his guns. He went home, took a few days off and began to think about his experience and his skills and how they could best be applied to other jobs in other companies.

Within two weeks, without raising a finger, he had two job offers from other companies, both paying substantially more than he was getting before, and both offering all kinds of opportunities that were vastly superior to the job he had walked away from. As soon as the word had gotten out in the marketplace that he was available, other company owners, having worked with him and his company in the past, were eager to open doors for him. As he moved down the corridor of life, he began to see possibilities that he had been missing completely by limiting himself to where he was.

If you want to be more successful faster, just do or try more things. Take more action; get busier. Start a little earlier; work a little harder; stay a little later. Put the odds in your favor. According to the Law of Probability, the more things you try, the more likely it is that you will try the one thing that will make all the difference.

I've found that luck is quite predictable. If you want more luck, take more chances. Be more active. Show up more often.

Tom Peters, the best-selling author of *In Search of Excellence* and other business books, found that a key quality of the top executives in his study was a "bias for action." Their motto seemed to be, "Ready, aim, fire." Their attitude toward business was summarized in the words, "Do it, fix it, try it." They realized that the future belongs to the action-oriented, to the risk taker.

Top people know, as General Douglas MacArthur once said, "There is no security in life, only opportunity." And the interesting thing is this: If you seek for opportunity, you'll end up with all the security you need. However, if you seek for security, you'll end up with neither opportunity nor security. The proof of this is all around us, in the downsizing and reconstructing of corporations, where thousands of men and women who sought security are finding themselves unemployed for long periods of time.

There is a "momentum principle of success," which is very important to you. It's derived from two physical laws, the Law of Momentum and the Law of Inertia, and it applies equally well to everything that you accomplish and fail to accomplish.

In physics, the Law of Momentum says that a body in motion tends to remain in motion unless acted upon by an outside force. The Law of Inertia, on the other hand, says that a body at rest tends to remain at rest unless acted upon by an outside force.

In the simplest terms, as they apply to you and your life, those laws say that if you stay in motion toward something that is important to you, it's much easier to continue making progress than it is if you stop somewhere along the way and have to start again. When you look at successful people, you find that they are very much like the plate spinners in the circus. They get things started; they get the plates spinning. They continually keep them spinning, knowing that if a plate falls off, or something comes to a halt, it's much harder to get it restarted than it is to keep it going in the first place.

Once you have a goal and a plan, get going! And once you start moving toward your goal, don't stop. Do something every day to move you closer toward your goal. Don't let the size of the goal or the amount of time required to accomplish it faze you or hold you back. During your planning process, break down the goal into small tasks and activities that you can engage in every day. You don't have to do a lot, but every day, every week, every month you should be making progress, by completing your predetermined tasks and activities, in the direction of your clearly-defined objectives.

And here's where the rubber meets the road. The most important single quality for success is self-discipline. It's the ability to make yourself do what you should do, when you should do it, whether you feel like it or not.

Let me break down that definition of self-discipline. First, it's the ability to make yourself do it. This means that you have to use strength and willpower to force yourself into motion, to break the power of inertia that holds you back. Second, do what you should do, when you should do it. This means that you make a plan, set a schedule, and then do what you say you'll do. You do it when you say you'll do it. You keep your promises to yourself and to others.

The third part of this definition is whether you feel like it or not. You see, anyone can do anything if he feels like it, if he wants to do it because it makes him happy, if he is well-rested and has lots of time. However, the true test of character is when you do something that you know you must do whether you feel like it or not—especially when you don't like it at all.

In fact, you can tell how badly you really want something, and what you're really made of as a person, by how capable you are of taking action in the direction of your goals and dreams even when you feel tired and discouraged and disappointed and you don't seem to be making any progress. And very often, this is the exact time when you will break through to great achievement.

Ralph Waldo Emerson once wrote, "When the night is darkest, the stars come out." Your ability to endure, to continue taking action, step-by-step, in the direction of your dreams, is what will ultimately assure your success. If you keep on keeping on, nothing can stop you.

If you have the discipline to practice the power of initiative, your eventual success is assured.

Morgan closed her phone with tears in her eyes. She knew what it was like to feel tired and disappointed. Too often she let others, and herself, remind her that she wasn't progressing anywhere. As if she wasn't stirred enough, this threw her over the emotional edge, but in a most touching way. The release of everything that had been bottled up for so long was finally making its way to the surface and it felt spectacular.

# Chapter 7

# UNQUESTIONABLE SUCCESS
# NOW O'CLOCK
# TAKE A CHANCE

"I'm sorry ma'am, but it looks like you have no collateral and no real business plan to back you up. It's a difficult time right now and I just don't see how we can finance this for you." The bank teller had a nametag that read Diane.

Morgan looked at Diane's tag one more time. "Diane, I don't have much of anything right now. I don't have collateral, no. I've never owned a house. I've never bought a new car. I've never really gone on a vacation. I don't have anyone to share my life with right now and all I have right now is this feeling that I have to do it."

Diane continued to listen to Morgan. Morgan couldn't tell if she was waiting for her to stop or genuinely concerned.

Morgan waited.

Diane looked at her computer screen again and back down at Morgan's application. Then she went to her drawer and pulled out a piece of paper. She scrolled her mouse as if she were searching for something. When she found it, she took her pen and scribbled down a name and a phone number and slid it over to Morgan. "I want you to call him."

"Who is this?"

"A friend. He'll help you. I'll let him know you will be calling."

Morgan took it graciously and lept out of her chair and went in for a hug, which was so unlike her normal character. "Thank you, Diane. Thank you so much."

"I don't know how much he can do for you, but he'll be able to help you." She nodded in receipt of the gratitude and tried to hide her shared excitement for this woman's dream.

"Good morning! This is Dwain Johnson." She felt at ease as soon as he picked up the phone.

"Hi Dwain, my name is--"

"Morgan!" Dwain answered immediately.

She smiled through the phone. "Yes. Morgan."

"Morgan, did you know that I have a weakness for chocolate and cream?"

"Well, it looks like you're talking to the right girl," she said, instantly energized by his voice alone.

"Morgan can you meet me at 7272 5th street in about an hour? Do you know where that is?" He was in motion.

"Um, yeah, you mean near the theatre?" Morgan was trying to picture the spot.

"That's it!"

"Um, ok. Is there a reason why I'm meeting you there?"

"You'll find out," Dwain said with an intuitive 'I know something you don't know' tone in his voice and then hung up.

Morgan dove into her closet in search of something with color. She needed it. She had no idea why she was meeting a total stranger in one hour or how he could help her, but she was intrigued and she was ready and if anything, she would be bright.

One hour later, Morgan found herself outside a rundown empty shop with boards and signs all over it. There were old moving signs, sale signs and available-for-rent signs. This wasn't what she had pictured as a meeting spot. She double-checked the numbers on the building and sure enough she was at the right place. She peeked in and then looked around at the adjacent places, just in case he gave her the wrong address. Or maybe this was a cruel joke played by the unbending bank teller. Could it be?

"Morgan?" There he was. "Great to see you!" Dwain said.

"Maybe not," Morgan thought.

"Well? What do you think?" he asked with his arms open wide.

"About what?" Morgan looked around.

"This fantastic place!"

"Huh?"

He pointed to the dark vacant building that resembled a rat hole. "This fantastic place for your bakery?" he repeated.

"Um, I think there's been some confusion."

"Confusion? What do you mean?"

"Well for one, I don't have the money right now to open a place and I'm trying to figure that part out and two…" She looked at the place, crinkled her nose Morgan style and shrugged as if no explanation was needed.

"Ah, c'mon, Morgan. Vision… confidence… and then it's unquestionable!"

"What is?"

"Your success." He said as if it was a no brainer and everyone should know this.

"My success is unquestionable?"

"Absolutely, but stop saying it as a question say it as a statement," he insisted.

"My success is unquestionable."

"Now, mean it."

"My success is unquestionable!" she said emphatically. She couldn't help but smile when she did.

"There you go!"

"Ok, great. Unquestionable success!" Then she looked around again. "But, what now?"

"First, remove the mental roadblocks and then get there." He reached in his pockets for keys and proceeded to open the doors to the decrepit space.

"And how do I do that?" She reluctantly followed him into the shop. "Whew," she said, holding her breath from the foul smells.

"Hmm. Yeah, no one's been back here in awhile to clean up." He looked around, not at all bothered by the smell.

"Looks like it need a lot more than a cleanup," she added.

Dwain spun around. "You do you want to open up a bakery, don't you?"

"I do," she agreed at once, realizing she sounded negative.

"It's got a kitchen in the back and all of the zoning is already correct. It used to be a deli, but the owner's wife passed away and then the place started to go downhill. No one from the family came to help and soon enough he went out of business. It's a little rough so it's going to take some elbow grease". Dwain handed her a piece of paper with the price break-down, financing terms, and the payment amount. "I can offer you this place for dirt-cheap. I bought it from the previous owner, with some creative terms." He was right. Cheap. But still, she didn't know how she would make her own rent next month, let alone make payments on another place, clean it up and start a business. She did appreciate the gesture, though.

"I wish I could. I mean. I guess once cleaned up, it could be great. The location is perfect, but . . . ."

"I haven't finished," Dwain interrupted.

"What?"

"You wouldn't have to make a payment for the entire first year!"

Morgan stopped her thoughts of walking out the door right there. "What? I don't understand."

"I told you I was able to structure some pretty creative terms when I purchased, right? Well, I can pass those terms on to you! Remember Diane, from the bank?"

"Yeah" Morgan listened.

"She had her own dreams of opening up a shop here for her and her sister, but her husband wouldn't support it, so she gave up."

"And that's why I'm here?"

"Yep."

"So, I would just need to get it cleaned up, But, then I need to worry about the--"

"Don't worry about that part yet," a voice from behind the room came through.

"What?" Morgan looked around.

"That you J?" Dwain called out.

"I'm here." He walked into closer view. He was tall and handsome and she now had a face to the voice that called out from nowhere.

"J and I have some projects we're working on together."

"You scared me," she admitted.

"I'm J. Massey." He held out his hand and laughed heartily. "Yeah, sometimes I have that effect on people." He looked at her sheepishly. "What's this I hear about you worrying?"

Morgan felt caught and she didn't even know why. She put her head down. "Oh, well I want to open a bakery and this is too good an offer to pass up, but I'm worried about the next step."

"What about it?" J looked as if this was new to him that anyone would worry about a next step.

"Buying the supplies, hiring people. I mean I don't really know what to do yet. I'm in my first six months of understanding this whole concept."

"And you're going to keep on learning. That's how it goes. But, you can't worry about the next step. You gotta think and take action at now o'clock."

"But, what happens when," she started.

"Nope. Don't think about that yet. Do what you gotta do now. Worry about the other stuff as it comes. Right now you need a place to start this business. You got it for a whole year right?" He looked over at Dwaine for approval who nodded back. "You can't afford to procrastinate. Know what you need to do and do it now and everything will follow. There will always be an excuse of why you can't do something. But figure out a way to get past that excuse and move forward."

"Wow. That's almost scary." Morgan took a deep breath.

"You know the best way to get over fear of anything?" J returned.

"Uh." Morgan was looking inside her head for the answer.

Before she could finish thinking Jay interjected, "Do it!" He nodded. "Period."

"What if I don't know my next step?"

J came closer to Morgan. He seemed used to getting this question. "Where do you want to be a year or two from now? How do you see this place?"

Morgan closed her eyes and imagined black and pink swirls along brass framed countertops. She pictured a full house with people smiling and laughing and enjoying decadence. She saw herself smiling at the regulars and offering them tastes. She could hear French melodies in the background. She saw a cash register overflowing with money and best of all, she saw fulfilled promissory notes encapsulated into a boxed frame. She told Jay almost as much.

"Normally, my clients tell me they see that they bought the building they wanted and we go from there, but ok. You've got a specific plan for this place don't you?"

Morgan giggled like a schoolgirl, "Yes."

"So reverse engineer your way to today. What comes before getting the people?"

"Being good at baking?"

"Ok. And then," he urged her on.

"Um, well I need the appropriate appliances and bake ware to make everything."

"Uh huh."

"I need to get the money to pay for all of that." She was thinking now as if she were reading a list on the wall.

"Go on." He supported her thoughts.

"Well, I'm going to need the kitchen to be cleaned and approved. Um, I'll need to get the place and clean it." She looked around and then back at J. "I guess I'll need to sign a tenant agreement?"

"You hear that Dwain?" J called to the front of the space then eyed the place. "Looks like you got yourself a tenant." Then he put his head in towards Morgan, "And I can't wait to bring my family."

"Thank you, J." She offered her hand, but he responded with a hug.

"Hey," he said. "I've got something for you. It's something very powerful and it reminds me every day that you have to take action, there's always going to be a risk." He walked over to his computer bag that was resting up against the tattered walls and pulled out a magazine that was already opened and folded to a certain page. Before he gave it to Morgan, he told her, "I usually keep this with me at all times. It's an older copy, so I can't get another, but I want you to have it." He handed it to her.

She looked at it, but turned it back to him. "Oh, I couldn't take that from you."

"Oh, yes you will," he said with a quirky attitude. "Besides I got that thing memorized in my head. Read it anytime you feel stuck. He's a pretty awesome dude."

Dwain walked in just then. "How about some coffee, Morgan? We'll sign some things and make dreams come true. Café la Claire? It's just down the - ."

"Oh, I know where it is."

She turned the key to her apartment door and took a moment as she walked over the metal threshold. Every day she walked through that doorway she was different and more improved. She felt she'd been locked up for so long at no one's fault, but her own. She absorbed the moment and licked the last bit of salt from her lips from the baked potato chips and tuna melt she ordered with her coffee. Inside a little brown bag was her *madeleine* cookie, which she would enjoy with a good article from another new friend, J.

She pulled out the chair to her kitchen dinette and dimmed the lights just low enough so she could still read. She lit a candle just next to her and began.

Take a Chance
by Three-time Olympian Ruben Gonzalez

The most successful people in the world are risk takers. As soon as they see an opportunity, they move quickly and make something happen. They have a special quality that sets them apart from less successful people. They take initiative in everything they do.

Successful people accept responsibility and take action when they see something needs to be done. They move quickly. They don't suffer from paralysis of analysis. They just do something. Anything that will get them closer to their goal.

By taking action - massive action - they build momentum and soon good things start to happen. One of my business mentors likes to say, "Most people need to think less and act more." Another of my mentors always says, "Done is better than perfect." Another way to say it is – implement now, perfect later.

Management guru Tom Peters says, "If you want to succeed, be willing to fail. To succeed big, be willing to fail big. To succeed fast, be willing to fail fast." He's absolutely right.

Successful people are willing to try different approaches to reach their goal. They are not worried about failing. They are just focused on the result. They just throw mud on the wall knowing that if they throw enough, some of it will stick.

They never focus on the approaches that didn't work. There's no time for that. Wallowing with self-pity is for losers. Winners simply learn from their mistakes and quickly try a different approach.

The faster they move, the more energy they have. The more different things they try, the more likely they are of succeeding. They make a game out of it. And they never take their focus away from the goal. Their attitude is – there is always a way. I will find a way. I will succeed.

A national survey of octogenarians revealed that their biggest regret in life was not having had taken enough risks. Think about that! What they're saying is they realize they did not live life to the fullest and they missed out. When you turn eighty you'll either be saying "I wish I had" or "I'm glad I did!" So go for it. Take a chance. Do something. You'll be glad you did.

Morgan folded the magazine up and put it into her purse to carry with her. She was well on her way to becoming that eighty-year-old, but fortunately she lost her job and found herself.

# Chapter 8

# BEAM OF LIFE
# SHIFT
# MIRROR REFLECTION
# APPLE TREE

Morgan had to remind herself today over and over again to not quit, to be faithful to her dream and to keep taking the chance. She read her articles, she boosted her own support cell and she sought John for guidance. She was in need of help to clean the space and she needed funds to order all that she needed to get her shop to opening day and the sooner the better. The time was now. She had a long list of people she wrote notes to and it took every bit of strength to ask them for help. While everyone offered immense support emotionally and morally, no one offered help financially. They were either tied into too many other investments or just couldn't swing it at the time with the current state of the economy, so they said. She couldn't blame them, though. After all, what had she done to prove that she was a viable investment? No one saw her as anything but a failure; especially compared to her younger sister.

She took a deep breath, but as each phone call resulted in a no, she was getting filled with more and more anxiety. She looked around at her apartment and questioned what she'd done. Soon, she wouldn't have a place to live. She had two more weeks until her next rent check would be due and most of what she had in savings was being spent on baking goods for her own pleasure, never mind customers. She would make it maybe one more month if she squeezed what she had left in savings and what she got as severance and then she would be done. And where would she go? Now, she would have the responsibility of this store that was filthy and in one year she would have to start paying rent. Her heart was beating faster and faster. The blood was rushing so quickly it became hard for her to breathe in a calm manner. She had to get out.

She frantically rushed out of her apartment and down the stairs. She didn't know where she wanted to go. First she would stop for some tea. Maybe that would help.

Beautiful chimes welcomed her as she opened the door. No one was at the counter. She assumed James was in the back or not there at all today. She decided to look around and pick the best medicine for her outrageously uncompromising nerves.

While looking at one tin, she noticed someone standing in the other corner of the store. She walked over to see, in the event that the person worked there. When she got a closer look, she saw a man with long black curls, holding a tin himself. He had a peaceful smile on his face. He wore a woven jacket that belled at the sleeves and looked to be made of hemp. His pants were of similar material. If she were to draw a picture of bliss, this man would be it. His feet were grounded and yet he seemed to be floating.

She cleared her throat. "Ah hem."

He didn't turn just yet.

"Excuse me?" She couldn't help herself. She assumed he did not work there, as he was much too intrigued with the teas.

He turned around, and as he made eye contact, his face broke into a broad, bright smile.

Morgan couldn't help but smile back, momentarily. "Do you know if anyone is working here today?"

He shook his head, put his right hand over his heart, and continued to beam at her. His eyes were penetrating, yet soft and gentle, and held her gaze. She waited. And waited. And waited. But, there was only silence. She started to feel uncomfortable, broke his gaze, and turned away. She continued to look at the teas.

As she read the labels, she suddenly felt a warm presence just behind her. She looked up and it was the same man. "Oh! You startled me." She laughed nervously.

"Aloha," he beamed at her. "Can I offer you a hug?" He said with a soft raspy voice.

"I'm sorry?"

"A hug." He smiled more warmly as he reached his arms out towards her and without waiting for her response, he went in for it.

"Oh," she awkwardly allowed the hug "Uh okay." She stood there with her arms stiff at her side while he wrapped his arms around her body and gently swayed in the slightest motion. She felt warm and so uncomfortable, until suddenly the discomfort started to fade and she felt as if her body were melting. She went with it. She gave into the feeling of a total stranger offering a hug and accepted it and even started to hug him back. Her fears and worries fled from her and she felt a soft, warm glow arise within her chest. The hug seemed to last an hour, but was only a minute at most.

When he pulled away, he looked into her eyes and took her hands. "Are you feeling lost?" He asked her with his gentle voice.

She just nodded.

"Be authentic with yourself. Empty your bucket of that worry and confusion. Then fill it back up with love and acceptance of yourself."

On any other day, she might have run from such a man. But, today, on a day when she felt so lost, so frustrated and so challenged, she also felt willing. Willing to accept the unexpected. "What's your name?"

"Arvin. Arvin Hsu," he replied.

"What do you mean, 'Be Authentic?'"

He smiled again. "Close your eyes… and take three deep breaths."

She started to comply.

He continued, "Follow each breath into your chest, into your heart. There, each breath dives into the core of who you are."

She followed the soft flow of her breath, imagined it milling around in her lungs, like a soft light, gathering in her lungs.

He said, "Yes, you are that. That core of your being. You are that. You are not your name, not your identity. You are not your job, not your career."

She concentrated on the soft warm feeling of peace that hadn't left her, and she realized that all her fears and anxieties of this morning didn't change how she felt.

"Fears are all stories about the future. No matter what happens, nothing can take away who you are at your core, your being, your light. Anxiety and worry cannot change who you are. So let them all go. You no longer need them."

She felt a tension relax in her shoulders as all her fears fled from her, and she settled into the present.

"You are a beautiful, spectacular being, gifted with wisdom, strength, and grace. Love and accept yourself, and fill all the space that used to be filled with fear and anxiety with that light: that wisdom, strength, purpose, and vision."

Morgan started to feel that same clarity come back to her again. Excitement about her café flooded back through her, and joy burst through her heart. She opened her eyes to find him watching him.

As he saw the delight in her eyes, he burst into melodious laughter, and exclaimed, "Yes. Yes. Exactly that!"

She couldn't help but join in. It felt like she was standing in her café already, laughing in exultation at her success, at her manifestation of her vision.

He put a hand around her shoulder and walked towards the exit of the café with her, laughing gently.

"Will I see you again, Arvin?" she asked as if she could use one of those hugs every day.

"Always," he answered. "Remember to surrender, to trust and to love. To surrender into your divine flow of creation, to trust yourself and the universe, and to love, to love yourself, your work, and all that you touch."

Just before turning away, he interjected, "Oh, and do me a favor?"

"Yes, of course," she said automatically.

"Always shine on!" He laughed as he danced away.

And just like that her beam of light left the store.

While the papers weren't completely finalized, Morgan felt so energetic that she decided she wanted to get her new bakery cleaned up and ready for its adventures. She called Dwain and he was able to get her the keys right away and clear it with the owner, who was more than happy to let the cleaning begin. She would need some help, though. She never reached out much to Alia Ott, who was an old friend. Whether it was because she was intimidated by her dedication and success, she wasn't sure, but she knew that she needed to take a chance every single day. After all, what was the worst that could happen? She'd already heard so many no's. She could at least complete the next step, which was to clean this place up.

She wrote a long email to Alia, whom she knew still lived in the neighborhood. She tried to justify her absence as a friend and then asked politely if she could use her help in cleaning. Alia replied with a quick "Yes, would love to. What time?"

She summoned two more girls she'd met through her baking class and in less than an hour, there were four of them with spray bottles, disinfectant, brushes, brooms, vacuums and mousetraps.

"I think it's going to be great!" Ishwari Jay said with her perfectly sweet French accent.

"I can't wait to help you decorate," Lori Taylor said, looking around.

"Oh, will you?!" Morgan was so excited. She walked over to her portable mp3 player and turned on French music to invoke the atmosphere. The girls were loving it.

"Reminds me of me and your sister playing in the yard with hats, gloves and red lipstick. We felt so French." They all giggled. Alia had been a friend of Morgan's younger sister, but when her sister left town, Alia and Morgan grew closer.

"Wow. And it took me this long to get here." Morgan sighed.

"No! Don't look at it that way. You weren't ready then," Ishwari added as she pulled out a garbage can to the center of the shop.

"What do you mean?" Morgan asked, pulling cobwebs from the ceiling.

"You weren't ready to step out of your head." Ishwari walked over to Morgan to hand her a garbage bag. "You were being a victim of life instead having the freedom to live it. And now you have found that. Now you are ready."

"Wait." Morgan stopped for a moment. "What do I do when I feel like a victim again? I mean just this morning I felt horrible and then suddenly I meet this amazing man who gives me this long deep hug and I feel like a new woman again." They all laughed and asked where they could find this man. She laughed with them. "But, seriously, it's like I go back and forth."

"That's okay," Ishwari said. "Just know how to make the shift each time and it will stick."

"I mean I love what you're saying. But, how do you shift, Ishwari?" Morgan needed to know now.

"Ok, let's take the word 'shift' and work through this." Ishwari captivated them all with adorable accent and valuable words. They were all eager.

"S – Say no to the status quo." She paused and looked at them and watched to see if they understood. They were with her. "H – hold off the inner critic."

They all shouted at this point as if they had a personal relationship with this inner critic person.

She giggled sweetly. "You musn't do it! That voice means nothing. Don't give it any importance!"

"Go on!" they all yelled to her.

"Okay okay. F – Follow the models of successful mentors." She looked to Morgan. "You have those?"

Morgan looked at each girl in the room with her. "Yeah, I think so."

"Cheers to that!" Lori held up her café latte and the girls followed.

"And T," Ishwari said with her eyes wide.

"T!" Each of the ladies was heavily involved.

"Take fierce action!" Ishwari took a bow.

The girls applauded her. "I'll do it." Morgan said slightly calmer than the rest.

Between sweeping, dusting, scrubbing and deodorizing, the girls were getting tired. Just as their ammunition was beginning to dwindle, Morgan's phone rang. She picked it up quickly without checking to see who was calling. "Hold on!" she called as she answered and fumbled to get the phone to her ear. "Hello?"

"It's mom."

"Oh, hi."

"I heard something about you getting a store. Maggie said she got a picture from you on her phone. She sent it to me. It looks God awful. Morgan, what have you done?"

"Oh, mom. Please. The last thing I need right now is for you to come down on me. This is my life. I'm not going to look for another average job that gives me a less than average life. I'm tired of it! And I love you mom, but if you're not going to support me in this then please don't call me anymore." She hung up the phone.     The women stood silent as they watched Morgan's cheeks get red.

"Good for you, hon. You broke the mirror," Lori said, tying her long blonde hair into a ponytail.

"What mirror?" Morgan looked around the floor for shattered glass.

"That damn reflection you had of yourself for so long." Lori only knew Morgan a short time, but could tell instantly that she was in the middle of a transformation.

Morgan sighed.

"Unfortunately, when we listen to all those naysayers, we start to believe them and become what they tell us." She looked up at Morgan who was standing on a ladder. "Until you know what you are you will attract what you're not. And by the looks of your ever-changing world, I think you know who you are. I'm proud of you for letting your mom know, too."

"Wow, Lori. Thank you for recognizing that," Morgan said.

"She may or may not change, but don't get hung up on what she says. Don't let it get you so angry. You have the choice to get upset or not, don't let others make that choice for you."

"You're right, Lori," Alia added with a smile.

"Look around you. That's your mirror. That's the reflection of who you are today."

Morgan took it all in and felt extremely proud and filled with joy to call such fabulous women her friends.

It was getting late and the women were ready to call it a night. The floors were sparkling and the walls were ready to be painted. The ceilings were clean of cobwebs and the place, while still empty and in need of color, had a new feel to it. Morgan was getting excited. She walked around and gave the woman a tour of what the place would like and what was in store. She had plans to make the entire bakery environmentally friendly, by using energy saving equipment and organic ingredients. They fell in love with her vision.

Lori and Ishwari were saying goodnight as they put on their sweaters and gave their hugs goodbye. They vowed to rejoice in celebration at their next baking class.

Alia was helping Morgan round up the last bit of trash. "Hey, Morgan?"

"Yeah?"

"You mentioned in your email that you were having a tough time with investors," Alia took a more serious tone.

"Oh, yeah, but you know I still have more people to call. I'm worried, but I'd be more worried if I did nothing. I really think, somehow, it's going to come together," Morgan said with a sweet smile.

"I'm sure of it. In fact, I don't how you feel about this, but I'd love to invest if you're open to it," Alia tested.

"Are you kidding me?" Morgan exclaimed.

Alia laughed at her excitement. "Well, there are only few stipulations on my end."

"Okay." Morgan was all ears.

"What do you think about creating a business where you can give back and still be profitable?"

"Um, sounds too good to be true?"

"It's not. It's actually what I promote with CHARITY INC and you're doing so many good things with yourself and you have good intentions with your business. I'd love to offer a little anecdote if I may."

"Alia. It would mean the world to me if you could help me create just that." She stopped for a minute and bit her lip. "But, do you think you could explain to me how it works."

"Absolutely!" They both took a seat on two empty bins. Alia had a great big smile on her face. "To put it simply. I believe in the apple tree."

"The apple tree," Morgan echoed.

"Yes. See, to successfully grow an apple tree, you need seeds, good soil, water, fertilizer and patience to grow a tree that produces apples."

"I'm with you." Morgan squinted at Alia and held on to each word she spoke.

"As you know and as you are finding out, it takes time to invest in creating something. Like the apple tree. It takes time creating an apple tree that has harvest."

"Okay." Morgan followed intently.

"With patience and nurturing, the tree becomes bountiful and produces fruit that not only helps sustain you with food to eat, but you can take the seeds and . . . ."

"Grow more apples trees," Morgan completed Alia's sentence as she nodded. She felt enlightened in that moment. She was getting it.

"And if you chop down the tree . . . ."

Morgan jumped in again, "The harvest will cease."

"You got it!" Alia laughed. "And that's what CHARITY INC is all about. We have an exponential model of creating businesses that do good and are growth oriented. See, most non-profits rely on donations to sustain them and if the donations stop, the organization will die. CHARITY INC likes to invest in the apple tree so we can grow more."

Beaming now, Morgan asked, "You would seriously consider investing in me?"

"You do meet our criteria. I mean you are a solid entrepreneur with a great idea and you are the type of 'seed' we want to nurture. We can give you the proverbial water and fertilizer you need to stay alive. Meaning we can mentor and give you the funding needed to get more customers. We then plant you in the right soil that will help you grow into your own healthy apple tree that can bear fruit."

"You mean profit?" Morgan clarified.

"Exactly. We put you in the right market that will yield you customers to sustain you and keep you growing. Then we take that excess fruit or profit and we create more businesses so we can do more good in a sustainable and exponential manner."

"So because my business promotes organic products and living and will give back, it would fit into your model?"

"Absolutely!"

"So let's see if I've got this. My business is the tree and the seeds are my ideas and products. I plant it in the right soil, which is the market and then I water it with customers. I use the fertilizer to keep it going by way of mentors and funding."

"That's right! It takes time to grow a healthy tree, but with the right ingredients it will flourish." Alia smiled and watched Morgan. "You know, I've been there."

"What do you mean?" Morgan asked.

Alia nodded, with a wistful expression.. "Not so long ago, I had a comfortable fundraising job that I dedicated nearly a decade of my life to. After learning the CHARITY INC model, I was confronted with a difficult decision—to leave something familiar or to start my own new social enterprise."

"And?" Morgan wanted more.

"The idea of moving on was a bit scary at first, but I have never once regretted making th choice to spread my wings and do exactly what I love. Now I get to live my passion of inspiring, like you, to create more sustainable businesses that do good."

Morgan took in the moment and saw herself fulfilling that model. She stood up and gave Alia a hug. Soon all the women were exchanging laughs and warmth. It was a good night for Morgan and another night that she would cross that threshold with heightened faith.

# Chapter 9

# INVENTORY

# THE POSITIVE

# FIERCELY LOYAL

# THREE ACTS

The first thing Friday morning, Morgan had to run into town to finalize the rental agreement of her shop. Once she officially became the tenant, despite the TLC already she gave, she felt it was time to get started. John encouraged her to go to her local book store to pick out some business books that would give her more understanding on opening a restaurant type shop. She decided to hit up her favorite outdoor mall and visit the large tri-level bookstore on the second level of the mall. The sun was blazing hot and there was a dry breeze in the air.

She walked into the store and could smell it right away. Books. Books that would have everything she needed. The first level hosted a coffee shop, where she knew she would be breaking for at least a biscotti or marble fudge brownie.

As she walked in further into the store, though, she could hear a speaking engagement. It was coming from the second floor of the store. She asked the woman standing closest to her if it was a free event. The woman assured her that as far as she knew it was open to everyone. Morgan was too curious now not to see what was happening, so, she made her way up the escalator. As she did the voice got louder and louder. She noticed that the people standing around this man speaking were completely glued to him.

"Inventory the positive. Society already does a good job of noting the negative. People. People tell us why we are not doing a good enough job. But, don't listen to society and don't listen to those people. Listen to you. Take inventory of the good because that is what empowers us and that is what will always stay with us."

The people were clapping as they watched this man walk on a small platform. Next to him was a life-size picture stand of himself smiling. His name was written on a banner just above. It said, "Empowering Minds with Eldridge DuFauchard."

"You all feel me, right?" They all cheered. "If we always think about the negative stuff, it will take away the empowerment. The economy is bad. Yeah, I already know that. So what? If you are empowered enough to know that our world is awesome, then the other stuff won't affect you as much. Make sense?"

Everyone clapped as the master of ceremonies for this event came back on stage and thanked Eldridge. He was immediately bombarded with people as he walked off the stage. Morgan just waited in the back. It seemed like an hour before the buzz started to die down. After everyone else had a chance to speak, Morgan walked up quietly to him. "Hi."

"Well, hello there!" He was still filled with as much as energy as he had on stage.

"I wish I could have heard your whole speech, but I came in just at the end. You really inspired me and I just wanted to thank you."

Eldridge grinned. He had a big smile and Morgan was warmed by it immediately. "Wanna know a secret?"

Morgan felt privileged. "Sure!"

"Few years ago if you walked up to me, I wouldn't even be able to say hi back to you."

"No way!" Morgan was shocked.

"You just commanded that stage. I would have thought you were doing this your whole life."

"One day I woke up and I realized that every thought I had and every feeling I had was determined by some other outside source. When I finally got that the happiness I was looking for was right there inside all along – all I had to do was take account of it? Man, it was like a rebirth of Eldridge!" His laugh was almost infectious.

"Just inventory the positive huh?" Morgan pondered.

"That inventory. Can't just do it once either," Eldridge added as he got his things together.

Morgan smiled.

"Alright, I'm outta here. Hope to see you again. Remember you have an empowering mind!" he called out as he walked away.

Morgan walked around and stopped to peruse the section John told her to visit. While in the business section she noticed a young man standing next to her. He was watching the books she picked up to read. She looked up and smiled. "Are you watching me?"

The young man laughed. "Well, yes."

She gave him a questioning look and then picked up another book. She could sense that he was still looking. Finally she looked up and said, "Ok, what?"

"Well, it's just that I see the books your picking and I'm dying to tell you what's worth reading."

"Oh" She felt relieved. "Okay. Please. What do you suggest?" She looked at the books and then back at him. "Wait, do you work here?" She looked around for a name tag.

"No, but I know this section well enough to."

"So, what do you suggest?" She grew eager.

"What exactly are looking to do?"

"Um, well, I'm starting a business. I've never taken a business course, or at least one that still serves my memory and I've got a coach that suggested I come here and look at the books so that I can get an idea of the process. I'm in the learning phase of my start-up."

"Well." He grabbed a few books off the shelf and handed them to Morgan. "These are great."

"Oh, okay."

"But, even better?"

"Yeah?"

"Strategic relationships," he said firmly.

"Is that what you do?" Morgan inquired.

"Every day." He leaned on one of the bookshelves. "I spend a lot of my downtime with the people I want to model after."

"So how do you do that?"

"Well let me ask you this. What do you want to do?"

"I want to open a world-class bakery and have it be known all over the world. Or at least my town to start." She smirked.

"Ok, great. Do you know anyone else doing something similar?" he asked.

"I don't think so. I mean I just know of the people at Café la Claire, my favorite café. I'm there almost every day. The owner is there a lot. Her name is Sophia I think."

"So, find out what Sophia does on her downtime. If she likes art, suggest going to a museum with her. Partake in new activities and learn from her. You'll have a new friend and a teacher."

"Here I am, practically there on a daily basis and I never thought to introduce myself."

He nodded. "Strategic relationships by Fred Becerra." He laughed.

"Fred?"

"Yep."

"Well, it was great meeting you Fred and--," she held up the books he suggested, "Thanks for these!"

Morgan got her books and started to walk back home. She checked her phone for any missed calls and there were three. She opened her mailbox and was about to listen, when a call came in from a mysterious number.

"Hi, this is Morgan."

"Hello Morgan, my name is Tom Thomson. I'm an old friend of your father's."

"Hi, Tom. Have we met before?" She wondered why he was calling.

"Well, it's been a long time and you were much younger when we first met. Your father and I served in the military together."

"Oh, how nice. What can I do for you Tom?"

"Your father told me you might be looking for help."

"Oh, no. I'm sorry, Tom. I hope my parents aren't trying to get you to hire me somewhere."

"No, nothing like that." He paused for a moment. "I met your father for lunch the other day. I was in town and he told me about your endeavors to start your own business."

Morgan was very interested now. Her father never even spoke to her about her wanting to start the bakery.

"He spoke very highly of you Morgan."

Morgan was silent. It was as if she found it hard to believe. Her father never really said much to her at all. She let him continue.

"After our stint in the military we worked together for quite a while until I left the company."

"Mmhmm." She wondered where this conversation was going.

"It wasn't until today that he forgave me for leaving," he finally said.

"What do you mean forgive you for leaving?" Morgan questioned.

"Well, he managed the company we worked for at the time and I was his employee."

It was starting to make sense but she still couldn't understand why he would be upset with him leaving.

"Your father was great to work for, but the time came when I felt I was done." His voice became softer. "Do you know how that feels, Morgan?"

"I do."

"There comes a point in your life when you realize that your worth is much more than what's on your paycheck."

Morgan stopped walking and sat down on a bench near by. "Go on."

"Your father knew that too, but he couldn't leave. Or at least he thought he couldn't." He cleared his throat. "I started to leverage my paycheck to create a life away from one, if you know what I mean."

"How'd you do that?" She listened to every word.

"Oh, I saved, invested in real estate, stocks, and all sorts of things that would alleviate any need for a regular paycheck. But, I stayed committed to the company for as long as your father said he needed me and I held true to that commitment."

"And then?" Morgan wanted more.

"He respected my loyalty. But then again, we haven't spoken for all these years."

"He wanted to do what you did Tom." Morgan knew why instantly.

"Well yes, I believe that's probably true. I can say this about your father. He cares for you deeply and he believes in you. He asked that I give you a call. He thought my words of advice might help."

Morgan was touched by her father's gesture. Though, she wished it came from him directly, she appreciated it nonetheless. "What's that, Tom?"

"Stay fiercely loyal, not just to others, but to yourself as well. There's a right and wrong way to do things in life. You need to believe and have faith in your own dreams to move forward. Your focus and commitment are key to everything you do."

"Your timing is just right, Tom. I'm so grateful you called." Morgan stood up from the bench and continued walking.

"Anytime. You call me anytime."

After reading a bit at one of the outdoor tables in the mall, Morgan decided it was time to go. It was getting late and she was exceptionally tired tonight. She wasn't sure why she was so tired, but she knew she needed a warm meal and a good night's sleep. She noticed some of the restaurants on her walk out of the mall and opted to stop for Mexican take out. As she pulled open the door, a couple was coming out and the lady and Morgan ran right into each other. Morgan's bag of books went flying everywhere. At the same time, her purse got caught on the door handle, while the heel of her shoe grabbed onto the thread of her long skirt. She slipped backwards and landed flat on her back.

"Oh, I'm so sorry!" the woman yelled.

"No, no," Morgan cried back. "It's not your fault. Complete accident."

"Well, you know what they say—"

Both women and the man said in unison, "There are no accidents."

"Let us help you." The man kindly offered Morgan a hand and the woman fetched her array of books.

"Wow, looks like someone's doing a lot of reading. Is this all for you?" the woman asked.

"Ha. Yes. I know it's a lot. I'm trying to figure out some things. Here I'll take those." Morgan offered to take them back from her. She went to place them in the bag, but the bag was now ripped.

"Where are you parked?" the man asked.

"Oh, I'm not parked anywhere. I walked. I was coming to pick up some food and . . . ." It spoke for itself.

"Go on in and order your dinner. We will get you another bag." He had an accent and it was very endearing.

"Oh, you don't have to do that. But, that's very kind, thank you."

When they came back, Morgan had ordered her food and found a comfortable chair to wait in. "Are you starting your own business?" the woman asked.

"Deborah noticed your books." The man laughed.

"Oops, I got nosy." She gave an innocent smile.

"Oh, it's okay. And yes. Yes, I am," Morgan answered.

"Just remember the three acts," Deborah said.

"The three acts?" Morgan asked.

"Misha, tell her."

"Oh, I'm Misha Elias by the way and this is my business partner Deborah Ives," he introduced.

"Hi." Morgan thought they were cute.

"We understand what it's like to start from scratch, so believe us when we tell you this, if you don't know where you are going, you won't get there," Deborah interjected.

"Yes, you need a road map," Misha added.

"A road map," Morgan noted.

"Act number two is commitment," Misha continued. "You need to be committed to the journey ahead, because let me tell you there will always be something that happens to get you off track, but you have to stay committed."

"Commitment, okay."

"Oh, I love this part." Deborah threw in, "Act number three is Act as IF. Act like you already have it."

"You mean like I already have my dream bakery that's getting rave reviews from everywhere?" Morgan laughed.

"That's it!" Deborah joined in. "Look if you take action as if you already are where you want to be, you will start doing everything that needs to be done to get you there."

"Really?" Morgan was surprised.

"We can't promise you that you'll succeed, but we can guarantee you will fail if you don't do these three things," Misha said.

"I guess there really are no accidents are there?" Morgan said to Deb and Misha.

"Morgan, your food is ready!" the host called.

"Well I'm so glad I ran into you. Literally!"

"Good luck to you!" Deborah and Misha said.

Morgan left the restaurant with her food in hand and books in a new bag in the other. Emotionally she felt on top of the world. Physically, she could begin to feel the effects of her fall.

# Chapter 10

# KNOW YOUR TRUTH
# NO LIMITATIONS
# THE REDHEADED WOODPECKER

The morning proved to be stiff and a yoga class proved to be impossible. Morgan's back was clearly unhappy. She fumbled through her list of doctors, dentists, homoeopathists, acupuncturists, massage therapists and chiropractors. There it was, Bill Janeshak. She'd heard about him through multiple happy clients and now it was her turn to visit. She never paid much attention to her body until it made a plea that she needed to. She called and even though he was quite popular, she was awarded an appointment that same day.

Sitting in the waiting room, Morgan grabbed a magazine and a cup of water. She had to shift around a bit to get comfortable in the chair, but it wasn't working. She was desperate to feel better. She looked up at the clock and realized she was still ten minutes early, so she did her best to be patient.

Coming out of the office was a woman that looked so familiar to Morgan. She watched her as she checked out at the front desk and made her next important move.

"Thank you, Sophia! We'll see you next time," the receptionist said.

Sophia! It was Sophia. Morgan couldn't place her because she was so used to seeing her in her apron at Café la Claire.

Sophia put her appointment card into her purse and smiled at Morgan as she headed for the exit door.

"Hi Sophia!" Morgan tried to stand up, but lost her balance. She laughed at herself.

"Now, where do I know you from?" She asked ignoring Morgan's almost fall.

"Your café! I'm there just about every day. I'd probably be there now, but . . . ." She gestured to her crooked posture.

"Oh well, Doctor Bill is just the best. He saved me from a brutal car accident. Got me back in tip top shape and I've been coming every other week ever since." Sophia was an adorable petite woman. She was older than Morgan.

"That's fabulous! I definitely need some help here."

"Well, you take care dear." Morgan watched, as if in slow motion, as Sophia headed towards the door. It was as if she was letting an opportunity walk right now. She wasn't sure if she should stop her or not. Sophia opened the door and let herself out and the door closed behind her. All the while, Morgan sat in dismay that she didn't say more.

"Morgan Kingsbury? Is that right?" A young girl came out with a chart and directed Morgan her way. At the same time, the doors to the office opened again.

"Do you know I think I left my glasses in the adjustment room? Will you be a dear and check?" It was Sophia.

The young girl agreed and told Morgan she'd be right back to take her to Dr. Bill.

"I'm starting to get forgetful," Sophia admitted to Morgan.

"Hey, Sophia?" This was her chance.

"Yes, dear."

"I want to open a bakery. I mean. I am. I'm opening a bakery of my own right on 5th street near the theater."

"Mr. Carlisi's old place?" Sophia was reflecting back.

"Yeah. His place. I rented it and I'm going to fix it up and open my own bakery." Morgan felt proud with her commitment to doing it instead of only wanting to do it.

"Well, won't that be a delight!" Sophia seemed genuinely pleased.

"I was wondering if you might be able to give me some pointers?" Morgan was hopeful.

"I'll tell you what. You come by early Monday morning and I'll show you what I do and how I got there." Sophia put her hands on Morgan's

"Really?" Morgan pleaded.

"Oh I'd love it!"

Morgan said her goodbyes to Sophia and continued with her visit to Dr. Bill. "So what'd we do here?" He asked, acknowledging her crooked stance.

"Well, let's just say, my books are a bit tattered. There's skirt strings on my shoe and I don't think I'll ever go unnoticed at the entrance of Star of India restaurant." She sat down gently on the table. "I had a clumsy fall."

"Ah, well, it happens to the best of us," Bill said as he pressed on Morgan's back.

He gently adjusted her spine back into proper alignment and explained the importance of maintaining her spine. He suggested a massage for her and some stretches to help alleviate the stiffness. All in all, he felt she'd start to feel much better after a few more rounds of adjustments.

"So you know Sophia?" Morgan asked as he rubbed her neck.

"She's great, isn't she?" he acknowledged.

"Yep. I'm sure hoping to learn a lot from her."

"Oh yeah?" He was focusing on her neck while he listened.

"Hey, can I ask you something?" Morgan said as Dr. Bill finished her exam.

"Sure can." He patted her to sit up.

She sat and turned to him. "How'd you get to be so successful with your practice? I mean what made you keep going?"

He gave her a great big beaming smile. "I knew my truth."

She nodded. "I guess you can't argue with truth, right?"

"Especially, when it's your own. Once you figure out what you are doing to serve other people you begin to create an environment that serves that purpose. So many people listen to what other's people truth is and they try to live their lives according to what someone else thinks. But, when you know your own truth, you become an expert at what you are good at and that's what serves others."

Morgan smiled. She couldn't tell whether it was her emotions making her body feel better or if it was her body making her spirit alive. It didn't matter either way. The healing was underway.

As the days went on, Morgan's life started to form a routine. Not in the sense that she did the same things every day, but in the sense that she did things with purpose. Her mornings were filled with either a walk to Café la Claire, a visit with John on her progress, cleaning the new shop and creating a wish list for supplies, learning the tricks of the trade with Sophia or reading on her deck. Whatever it was, she felt productive. There was good reason to get out of bed every morning. It was almost as if she was in love. Like she was walking around happily in love and yet what she was in love with was life.

She finally had things to do on her calendar that were strictly for fun. Baking classes expanded her mind and got her creative juices flowing. After each class, she met with her new friends for night cap or dinner and sometimes, even a movie.

It was last night that really engaged her in a way she hadn't been engaged before. Lori, Alia and Ishwari invited her to the town's biggest theater where a special treat would ensue.

When they took their seats and the curtains went up, there was nothing but a blank stage with one microphone. The audience was still, until he walked out. Brian Roman. Handsome, full of cheer and charm, Brian Roman stepped out onto the stage and opened his mouth.

As soon as the first note came out, Morgan was in trance. From Sinatra to Dean Martin, the guy took the audience on a trip they didn't want to come back from.

When the ladies stood up, they could see Morgan had a silly grin on her face. "I have to meet him!" She could barely contain herself.

"Oh well, you're lucky. I happen to know him," Lori stated.

"Oh my gosh! Please introduce me."

After the hustle and bustle of the crowd getting CDs autographed, Morgan finally got her introduction. Brian first gave Lori a big hug and kiss and then opened his eyes wide to meet Morgan. "It's a pleasure to meet you," he said with such kindness.

"You're amazing," was all she could say. "How do you do it?"

"Ah, well I keep it alive."

"You really inspire me." Morgan was like a nervous thirteen-year old.

"Morgan's opening up a French pastry shop. She's absolutely incredible." Lori shared.

"Congratulations," he said.

"It's been a dream of mine. It's what I love."

"And don't let anyone stop you. I'll tell you something. There are no limitations when it comes to what you're passionate about. If this is what you love Morgan, keep it alive and go for the top. As long as you believe in it, it will happen." He said, "It's easy when people are applauding you on stage or on your opening day. But real life will always be there. There will be times when things don't go your way, but if you focus on the dream and know what you are striving for, it will work itself out and bring you closer." He spoke to her with such kind words.

Lori smiled as she watched Morgan soak in the words of wisdom. Morgan knew there would be challenges. She could see it now, but she really felt the commitment now to keep moving and keep it alive no matter what came along. Seeing the people around her achieve dreams and experience success despite any hard times they had to face was proving to her that no matter what, there was no reason to stop.

Morgan played Brian's CD as she drifted off to sleep. The morning came too soon and with it a loud knocking noise. At first she thought it was someone at the door. But when she checked, no one was there.

Since she was already up, she decided to move on with her day. She brushed her teeth and headed to the kitchen to make a hot cup of tea. She did some stretches on the floor while she waited for the kettle whistle. Knock – Knock – Knock. There it was again. She got up and looked through the peephole, but still saw nothing. She shrugged it off, continued making her tea and sat down at the computer to check her email.

Yep. There it was. She knew it would be coming soon. An email from her bank, notifying that her that her account was overdrawn. Panic set in.

She took another sip of tea to calm her nerves. Knock – Knock – Knock. "Where is that coming from?" she said aloud. She searched for the source again and there, outside her bedroom window was a red-headed woodpecker. He was perched on the side of the big oak tree that dominated her view. She returned to her computer and looked at the email again. The panic came back.

Knock – Knock – Knock. Suddenly she smiled as the knocking triggered a memory. "The woodpecker," she thought.

Morgan remembered meeting Tim Campbell at a networking party her company required she attend. They were sitting next to each other at the rooftop bar and started talking. He asked why she was there; she explained that she was forced to attend by her boss.

"Do you like your job?" he asked.

"The truth?" she questioned, not sure how much she should reveal.

"Please." He waited.

"No."

"So, why do you do it?" he persisted.

"Well, I need a paycheck," she said reluctantly.

"So, you allow other people and fear to influence your choices." It was more of a statement than a question, and she could hear a challenge in his voice.

"I'm sorry? What do you mean by that?" Morgan asked defensively.

"Well, if you allow others to dictate your life's path, you will not be living in abundance. Staying in a job you don't enjoy, only because you are fearful of not having enough money, is living with a scarcity mentality. Every decision we make is based on whether we believe in scarcity or abundance," Tim shared.

"So, all of my current choices in life are based on scarcity?"

Tim just raised an eyebrow and let her silently answer her own question.

Looking back, Morgan now had a better understanding of what Tim meant.

"Let me give you an example using a red-headed woodpecker," he continued.

"What?" She laughed.

"Have you ever seen a woodpecker storing acorns in the holes of an oak tree?"

"Well, yeah." She was curious now.

"Did the woodpecker seem worried about securing the acorns for himself? Did he somehow lock them up, making sure no one else could take them? Of course not. Do you know why?" he asked her.

She shook her head.

"That red-headed woodpecker only lives in abundance. Nature has programmed him to believe there will always be enough."

She had talked with Tim for quite a while that evening about scarcity and abundance, but had never really applied the concept to her own life, until now.

Morgan returned to the window and pondered the abundance of the oak tree. She realized the woodpecker had been there for some time, but she had never been aware of its presence. She suddenly awakened to the understanding of what abundance truly meant.

Her bank account balance didn't matter; it was a temporary issue. She just needed to change her mindset and then anything would be possible. Her bakery wasn't just a dream; it was a burning desire that would become a reality, if she allows it to happen. She could now see the choices she had made over the years that kept her from achieving the success she deserved.

Knock – Knock – Knock. She never could have imagined the impact a little red-headed woodpecker could have to shift her beliefs and change her life.

# Chapter 11

# GO SCREW UP

Morgan just finished licking the last envelope of her grand opening invitation. Her plan was to send them out after *La Vie Belle Patisserie* was completely ready to be seen. But, there were still chairs that hadn't been shipped and paintings to be hung. There were mugs and serving plates that hadn't yet been delivered.

She'd never done this before and even with all the help from her new mentors and friends, she was still in a state of disarray, but overwhelming excitement. In her efforts to remain environmentally friendly, she met two more acquaintances of Alia who were eager to donate/invest in her business. As each moment came to the fight or flight point, she kept fighting and here she was about to realize a dream, but would she mess it up?

After the invites were mailed and signs were posted, the grand opening of *La Vie Belle Patisserie* would soon be here. Just days before the big day, a man came walking by that morning as she was organizing display trays and setting up a small stage area for Brian Roman to sing on her grand opening, as he so generously volunteered.

"When will you be open?" he asked poking his head in the cracked door.

Morgan walked over with a big banner in her arms. "I was just about to put up the sign. August 13th is the date."

"I do love the French."

"Well you must come then!" she invited.

"Can I give you some advice?" He had southern written all over his voice and a smile to match it.

"Ha! Is it that obvious that I need it?" She came back.

"No no. But, I will tell you this." She waited. "Go screw up!"

They both started laughing. "Well, it might not be that hard!"

"You do it. You know why?"

"Why?"

"Because you're doin' something!"

"You're being serious aren't you?" She wasn't laughing anymore. He shook his head and she gestured him to come in. "Can I get you lemonade or ice tea? It's all I've got in my fridge as of now."

"I'd love lemonade, thank you." He found a seat at one of the tables. She came out not long after and joined him.

"You've been on quite a journey to get here, haven't you?" he asked her.

"You can tell that?"

"I can look around and see what this means to you."

"Yeah, well I'm nervous. I've come a long way to get here, but I still feel nervous about where I'm going."

His name was Doug Bench and she told him of her journey and how it began.

"Morgan, I'm going to tell you something and I hope you do something with it, because it's very valuable." She leaned in with great intent while sipping her own lemonade.

"It doesn't matter if you consciously don't think you can reach your goals."

"Why?" She took the straw out of her mouth.

"Because five sixths of your brain does believe it."

"I'm not sure I get it."

He sat upright and leaned in to her more. "When you give your brain pictures, it reacts and it will move you toward realizing those pictures. Do you follow me?"

She tried to grasp this. "You mean what I think about and what I visualize is what my brain tells me to do?"

"Right. So if you're sending pictures to your mind that you might screw up at making this happen, you're brain at least sees you trying to make it happen. You're going to go in that direction no matter what. At least you're doing it, right?"

"Oh, I get it. I get it!" She was excited now.

"You've been visualizing this place haven't you? Sending your brain pictures of what you want it to look like." He pointed to everything around them.

"Well, yeah, I guess I have."

He smiled and stood up. "You keep those pictures up of what you really want. And don't be afraid to screw up. It's ok!"

Morgan sighed with relief as Doug walked out the door. With each person she met along her journey she added a promissory note. She kept a record of every person she wrote a promissory note to and wondered how many, if any, kept them and remembered them. It didn't matter either way to her, she made that commitment to them and to herself.

The day finally arrived. She was happily awakened by the redheaded woodpecker. She stood up and stretched and walked to her bathroom where she saw her reflection. She had color in her face. Her nails had grown back in and she was wearing pink pajamas. She had a French style sundress festooned with beads and ribbon. It was perfect. She felt full of life as she put it on and saw how it reflected her excitement.

She headed to the shop early enough to get everything set up. Friends offered to help and while she would have accepted, there was something sacred about her putting in the final touches and opening the doors on her own.

As the minutes approached, she peeked through the velvet curtains she had hung herself, but didn't see a soul in sight. Did they forget? Would they be here? Did she have the wrong time? Why was no one yet there? There was one knock on the door after she closed the curtains. It was Brian. She opened the door with urgency and hugged him right away. He was the first person to see the finished bakery.

"Wow," was all he could say. He proceeded to set up on the tiny stage she appropriately set for him and with seconds to go, she said, "Well, whether they're here or not, I'm officially open for business!"

She swung open the doors and there they were. One after the other. Faces she knew were coming in with bottles of champagne and smiles. Lori, Alia, even Raelyn were there. Sophia and even Dr. Bill came scanting in.

The music started to play and Brian's voice, the smell of *pain au chocolate* and rich coffee filled the air. It was a party and it was all in honor of Morgan Kingsbury, owner of *La Vie Belle Patisserie*.

She looked around at the beauty that surrounded her and sighed with relief. Amid all the hubbub, she felt a distinct tap on her shoulder. "Dan!" She yelled. "You came!"

"I wouldn't miss it for anything." Dan said. "Sure is nice looking at a leader."

"I fueled myself with the right stuff." Morgan smiled and gave Dan a hug.

"Congratulations girl. I'm proud of you."

Morgan watched Dan walk off into the crowd, remembering that he was one of the first people that caused her to think differently.

She smiled to herself with appreciation and then turned her attention to welcome her small staff and their first live day as they threw on aprons and served with delight. The pastries were exquisite and the atmosphere a dream.

Then there in the back stood her sister, her father and her mother. It was as if the music stopped playing for a brief moment as she made her way to them.

Maggie grabbed her instantly, "My big sis. You did it! You really did it."

She hugged Maggie and then looked to her parents who handed her two cards. She took them and slipped them into her apron. "Thank you, mom. Thank you, dad." She took their hands, "Thank you for coming. It means the world to me."

As the night came to an end and Morgan's first official day of business closed, Morgan said her last goodbyes to the guests. She sent her staff home after a job well done and shed a tear for her attempts at screwing up. Everyone she knew showed up. After forty-two years, Morgan was finally living.

She headed back to her small office and on the table were loads of cards. She first opened the card from her mother and father. Inside she found her promissory note and a note from her parents that read, "We are so proud of you." She opened the other cards one by one. With the cards of praise and support, she found her promissory notes. The cards reinforced her success. "We knew you could do it." "We believe in you, Morgan." "We never doubted you, Morgan." The praises rolled in.

She walked over to the empty boxed frame where she'd hoped she could display them one day. Here she was fulfilling every single promissory note. She placed them in the box and closed the lid. She took one sip of champagne, picked up a pink cupcake, and turned out the lights. "See you in the morning."

# Co-Author Biographies

**Donna Jean Beccia** is an expert in transformation. For four decades, Donna has been performing and teaching music, including being featured guest artist on "The Hour of Power" international television program, and a national competition winner. Along with being a contributing author and music critic for "The Arts in Orange County" newspaper, she also ran an entertainment-booking agency for 28 years. During the majority of these years, Donna was suffering with a mystery medical condition that was extremely painful and debilitating. The main thing that sustained her through that pain was the fact that she was living her passion, doing what she loved to do, which was music.

The medical field offered Donna no solutions to getting relief from the pain. She had been poked and prodded for years, with hormone injections, experimental drug therapies, continual x-rays and medical tests, and she continued to get worse and worse. In desperation, she began to read everything she could get her hands on, in the area of holistic healing. This process birthed a brand new passion for Donna, and she transformed her own life, to be pain-free, healthy, and joyful. In 2001, she became board-certified as a holistic health practitioner, so she could pass along to others the effective secrets to transformation.

Donna now sees clients individually, and corporately, to assist them in transforming their own lives, holistically addressing physical, emotional and spiritual avenues to improvement. She has walked through the process in her own life, and she uses her experience and strong intuition to show people the road-blocks to their well-being, and the simple and effortless ways to victory.

If you want your life to be joyful, and vibrant, let Donna assist you. She is passionate about helping people achieve their inherent greatness. Donna is available for individual sessions, or for speaking engagements at corporate functions, or retreats. She can be reached at www.donnabeccia.com or 800-211-3388

**Fred Becerra** is often described as somewhat handsome, kind to a fault, and a little bit of an outsider. A fan of challenging tasks since he was very young, Fred became an Eagle Scout, an NCAA distance runner, a martial artist, a biochemistry graduate, a science teacher, a top ranked multidisciplinary tutor, and running coach. Currently Fred brings his value into the world by leading a growing and ambitious marketing team in the financial services industry helping every sort of individual and institution manage and save their money while minimizing their tax profile. In his spare time, Fred enjoys giving back by developing droid applications designed to help teachers with his friends Ek Tong Ear and Tai Duong, and is working on a children's book to teach kids the value of running, good sportsmanship, and the quirkiness of life with his 'ole pals Nadia Roldan and Francisco Gutierrez. In his rarer moments he can be seen entertaining ladies, people-watching, reading, drawing or working out. Fred is grateful to all of his mentors who made it possible to get to this point in his life. One of those mentors is Tim Campbell who is featured in this very same book.

He looks forward to helping your family, business, charity or institution to getting to their dreams and goals in the very best way possible. He can be reached at 562 230-7682 or misterfredwfg@gmail.com.

**Doug Bench**, MS JD AAAS, is a noted educator, motivational dramatist, humorist, author, trainer and speaker, specializing in brain science-based performance and achievement systems. Armed with two degrees in Physiology and a Doctor of Law degree, Doug has spent the last nine years, after the death of his mother from Alzheimer's, researching and analyzing the findings of over 800 recent cutting-edge neuroscience (brain science) research studies and books to develop easily usable skills and techniques to maximize the life-long health, fitness and performance levels of the human brain. He has presented this exciting revolutionary brain science-based advanced achievement information to nearly 200 groups and a quarter million people in his seminars, speeches and books to rave reviews for the results his information has created for greater productivity, greater achievements, performance levels and overall brain health.

Doug is the owner and CEO of The Brain Training Academy, a Professional member of the American Association for the Advancement of Science, as well as the National Speakers Association, the International Speakers Network and various civic organizations. Doug has published the first two books in his series called The Brain Apples Blueprint, all based on recent cutting-edge brain science research discoveries:

*Revolutionize Your Brain—Kiss Your Old Brain Goodbye How to Apply Brain Science Techniques to Advance Your Achievements.*

*Do It Yourself Brain Surgery: Non-Invasive! 101 Brain Science Based Strategies to Implant in Your Brain Right Now for Awesome Brain Fitness and Performance!*

Doug can be reached at 352 562-5703 or doug@brainapples.com.

**Tim Campbell** has been a personal money manager for the past ten years investing his time, knowledge and passion for finance into his clients, to ensure that they and their families are protected and provided for. Throughout his career he has been a corporate executive, small business owner, inventor with multiple patents and trademarks and a published author. He is a professional speaker, speaking to audiences nationwide. He is an on-air TV personality for the sport fishing industry and has been featured regularly on broadcast radio stations covering various topics for multiple industries. He is currently working on a book project, The Red-Headed Woodpecker, where he compares the difference between scarcity and abundance and how it affects the choices we make on a daily basis. Follow the progress at www.rhw-inc.com or connect with Tim at tim@rhw-inc.com

**John Carmona** has been a savvy businessman since the age of four. His first business venture was as a banker. With the philosophy that "a penny saved is a penny earned," John provided small but essential loans that yielded high returns on investments. Today, John is an entrepreneur with a diverse business portfolio. His personal and professional motto is "failure is not an option." Discovering a natural talent for Sales at the tender age of 15, John quickly learned that he had both the talent and people skills combined that would enable him to succeed in business. Eventually, at the age of 23, this belief led to his being named the youngest Finance Manager in the Western Region for a leading international Automobile Manufacturer. The knowledge that John acquired during his tenure in the automotive industry allowed him to parlay that expertise into a multi-million dollar credit consulting business. Over the years, John has learned that unbridled determination and focus are the keys to greater success. As a Credit expert, John has the pleasure of inspiring, motivating, and educating people. He enjoys helping others define and achieve their personal dreams and goals.

Mr. Carmona's personal interests include family, diamonds and Fine Art. He is a dedicated and devoted family man to his wife Carole and their two children. He is also a diamond grader of rough and polished stones certified by the International Gemological Institute (IGI). He currently dabbles in Fine Art. Contact John at jpconsulting@yahoo.com.


**Deborah Clark** was a registered nurse for 32 years and has worked in the operating room for most of that time. At 55 years old, she is finally realizing her dream of being self-employed. She has two home-based businesses: internet affiliate marketing and equity options trading. Deborah lives in Yuma, Arizona, with her life and business partner Forrest May. She has three children,

Tina, Joshua, and Caleb, and two grandchildren, Elizabeth and Ella Ruby. Deborah can be reached by email at deborahclark5556@gmail.com.

**Eldridge DuFauchard** came from a humble background, raised by a single mother in Los Angeles California. It was during his second year in college when he began to feel out of sorts. He was diagnosed with a social dysfunction known as Social Anxiety Disorder. This plagued his life for twenty years, and it kept his true self bottled up inside his mind like a dense fog with no way out.

He fought tirelessly for many years to reverse the Social Anxiety Disorder, and overcame what has now become his power. His dedication to re-program his subconscious mind has assisted him in discovering his true purpose and passion in life, and that is to assist other people discover their purpose so they too can live a life of abundance, fulfillment, passion, and joy. Eldridge's passion shines when he speaks and connects to others because he loves so openly and shares his truth with everyone who crosses his path. He truly loves to make a difference in everyone's life and continues his own personal journey to creating heaven on earth for everyone who chooses to participate in making our world a more joyous and peaceful place. He can be reached at eldridge.dufauchard@gmail.com.

**Misha Elias** was born and raised in Mexico City, Mexico. He came to the United States in 1990 when he was 20 years old. As many immigrants, he came to the country looking not for a guarantee of success, but for a chance to succeed. Being an illegal immigrant, he couldn't register for school so he learned to speak, read and write the English language on his own. He worked through several "mediocre" jobs until in 1994 when he found a job at a car dealership. He started as a sales person and became a Finance Manager within nine months of employment. He held that position for 13 years, making over six figures a year. While the money was good, he realized he had no time to spend with his family. He learned that if he wanted to gain free time and increase his financial position, he would need to go into business for himself. He also learned that in order to achieve dreams, you need determination and guidance from other successful people in order to create success. Misha became a US Citizen in 2002 and is now a successful Real Estate Investor and Entrepreneur. He coaches and helps people to find the same opportunity to succeed in their lives.

You can reach Misha at 714-494-6438 or misha@mdinvestmentsolutions.com.

**Lane Ethridge** was born and raised in Rockville, MD. He was one of three boys who were raised by loving, nurturing parents. As a three-sport athlete, Vice President of his class and top 5% academically, he quickly learned the balance between fun and work. Lane attended Virginia Tech and was recognized as an outstanding student, graduating with honors. He won the intramural racquetball championship and started two philanthropies that still exist at Virginia Tech. Lane will forever be a Hokie. Upon graduation, Lane taught in the Montgomery County school system. He was as much a student as he was a teacher. He found his true passion as an entrepreneur and invested in his P.H.D - Personal Happiness Development. He believes that mentorship is a way to gain success with less pain. He became a full-time real estate investor, accumulating over $52 million in properties in the first two years. He now applies his skills to educating others about the power of building a business and the key principles to financial independence. His passion is teaching people how to "Nourish the Streak!"

Lane is an active member of his church and founded F.I.T. for the Kingdom - a group designed to help others deepen their faith through fitness in order to be transformed leaders who impact the lives of others. Lane promotes God, Family, Health and then business. He is passionate about helping others create a more fulfilling life and helping them "Nourish the Streak."

Learn more about Lane at www.LaneEthridge.com or his Facebook page www.facebook.com/LaneEthridge. He can also be reached at (240) 401-9742.

**Kent Georgi** believes in the paying it forward mentality and helping others. He educates himself with the expertise and experience of mentors performing successfully in the niches of business he would also like to be successful in. His pay-it-forward compassion assists him in helping others to reach their goals as well as his own. He is an expert at social media presentations for local businesses and assisting the real world with financial planning. An uninhibited entrepreneur, Kent demonstrates the ability to think outside the box and find revenue streams in the most unlikely of places. His service to the US Military gave him the discipline. His dedication to learning gives him freedom. Kent has developed a free-thinking entrepreneur mentality that blurs the idea of boundaries when it comes to business opportunities. Kent has moved from humble military service to a real world, real people financial planning industry. He assists anyone in finding the best investments and future financial tools. Working with the Make a Wish Foundation and local Children's Hospitals is Kent's way of giving a part of himself to the young futures of our country. Some of Kent's endeavors include speaking engagements for finding a soul mate, social media in San Diego, All Things

San Diego, Healthy Blue Planet and TransAmerica Financial Group. Kent can be reached at allthingssd@gmail.com.

**Gary Goldstein** specializes in brokering brilliant people and inspired ideas. An author, consultant, storyteller and celebrated Hollywood film producer, Gary has produced some of Hollywood's biggest box-office hits, including among others *Pretty Woman, The Mothman Prophecies, Under Siege,,* and its sequel. His films have generated well over a billion dollars in worldwide revenue, receiving multiple Academy Award nominations, People's Choice Awards, a Golden Globe and various other honors. Gary had entertainment beginnings. Music was his early passion. As an undergraduate and the youngest A&R rep ever for Columbia Records, Gary also produced all the concerts and cabarets on and for the UC Berkeley campus. And then it was from San Francisco to Hollywood for Gary. Given his love for the power of story, Gary couldn't resist the siren call of the film business. Abandoning law practice in San Francisco, Gary headed south to Los Angeles, quickly recognizing his early experience in the music trade was perfect preparation for the competitive and exciting world of film and new vistas ensued.

Gary also counsels early-stage and established companies poised for greater growth – bringing to bear the same agility, innovation, speed and story-telling strategies that underscore success in Hollywood - to help create stronger teams, brands, leadership, advisory boards and strategic partnerships, as well as sales and marketing messages, and bolster bottom line revenues.

Gary attended UC Berkeley and earned his J.D from Golden Gate University School of law. You can find more information on Gary at www.garywgoldstein.com.

**Ruben Gonzalez** is a Three-Time Olympian and a national luge champion. A peak-performance expert, Ruben knows how to achieve success again and again. As a master storyteller, he uses his Olympic experiences to inspire audiences to think differently, to live life with passion and to have the courage to take the necessary steps toward their goals– to push beyond their self-imposed limitations and to produce better results! Ruben was chosen for the way he embodies the Olympic Spirit and for inspiring others to reach new heights. Armed with the same energy and dedication that he put into his athletic career, Ruben brings to audiences of all sizes and backgrounds a truly unique, truly memorable performance that teaches as it entertains, and inspires as it motivates. Ruben can be reached at www.olympicmotivation.com

**Randy Hausauer** is a real estate investor and a network-marketing entrepreneur. Randy lost his father at the age of sixteen and it was by the grace of God, a loving mother, and a number of coaches and mentors who cared enough to give of themselves that life turned out so positively for him. After graduating from college with a degree in Financial Investments and Real Estate and in what can only be described as Divine intervention, he became a Long Beach Police Officer where he worked for nearly 29 years. It was during that time that he saw the best and worst in humanity and made a conscious decision to do whatever he could to make a difference. Because of his personal experience of losing his father at a young age, along with the positive experience that he had with his coaches and mentors, he developed a passion for coaching and mentoring youth, which still continues today. He believes that it takes a village to raise a child and that it is the responsibility of everyone in that village to make a difference and bring about positive change. He also subscribes to the Chinese Proverb, which states, "Give a man a fish and he will eat for a day. Teach him how to fish and he will eat for a lifetime." Lastly, a saying that he has become fond of is, "YOU were born to change someone's life... Don't waste it!"

Randy has the honor and privilege to work with many athletes, actors, and successful business people through Athletes and Entertainers for Kids/911 for Kids. Most notably is the work that he does with former super model turned business mogul, Kathy Ireland, and her Teen Mother Mentoring Program and with former Los Angeles/ Oakland Raider all-pro wide receiver and Heisman Trophy winner Tim Brown and his Mentor Mini Football camps for disadvantaged boys. If anyone is looking to give time, treasure, or talents to worthwhile programs for youth, please contact Randy. And of course, Randy is always open to discussing business opportunities in real estate or network marketing. Randy can be reached at randy.hausauer@gmail.com or by telephone at 562-480-5582.

**Michael S. "Boot" Hill** is a multi-company owner, successful real-estate investor, screenplay writer and movie-maker as well as an aspiring science fiction author. A native Ohioan, he holds a BS in Aeronautics from Miami University and a MS in Public Administration from Golden Gate University. He entered active duty with the U.S. Air Force in 1976 and retired as a Colonel in 2005. He flew single-seat fighter combat aircraft for over 25 of his 29 years, with 45 combat sorties during Operation Desert Storm in the A-10 attack aircraft. Colonel Hill is currently working as a defense contractor for the Defense Advanced Research Projects Agency (DARPA) in Arlington, Virginia where he works to usher highly advanced technologies into the Air Force. He lives in Alexandria Virginia with his wife Genette, also a retired Air Force Colonel. He can be reached at A10BootHill@aol.com or 703-535-6868.

**Arvin Hsu** is a child of this Earth, blessed by the Divine. He is a healer, a teacher, a student, a servant. The healing of our world requires that each of us, man, woman, child, step up and claim our authenticity, surrender into The Divine Flow, and celebrate joy, passion, love. Arvin exists to facilitate this, for himself, his soul family, every person, and the world. He holds a doctorate in Cognitive Psychology, is the founder of ecoProcity, has 15 years experience with startups, and has lifetimes of experience walking the jagged, brilliant, and ecstatic path of Life, Love, and Sacred Truth. Arvin can be reached at arvinhsu@gmail.com.

**Deborah Ives** owned a vending machine company prior to becoming a Real Estate Investor and Entrepreneur. Looking back "the vending machine company owned her." She went 12 years without taking a vacation or any time off. As a single mother, she desperately wanted time to spend with her two sons and grandchildren but the company wouldn't allow it. She wanted TIME FREEDOM! Now, she has time to travel and enjoy life at its fullest! Recently remarried and a mother of 11 children and grandmother of 12 grandchildren, Deborah now receives the ability to live a richer life in every aspect due to her current business. Deborah can be reached at deborah@mdinvestmentsolutions.com or 714-900-5708.

**Bill Janeshak** is the Director of one of Southern California's busiest Wellness Clinics, located in Yorba Linda, California. With passion for educating the public on achieving their optimum health goals, he leads a team of world class practitioners in helping people get out of pain and stepping into their dreams. He found this passion after suffering through childhood with a seizure disorder that was alleviated by Chiropractic, thus changing his outlook on life forever.

Since that time he has never slowed his enthusiasm for learning, having completed post graduate studies in Chiropractic, neurology, kinesiology, biomechanics, ergonomics, rehabilitation, and functional medicine. By combining his knowledge of all of these disciplines with an extraordinary team, the patients get extraordinary results. It is not unusual to see professional athletes, celebrities, and well-known business leaders in his office. Dr. Bill always says "To be at the top of your game, you need to be at the top of your game."

Dr Janeshak is a practitioner, corporate and public speaker, and author with a focus on health care and human performance. He lives on a small farm in Norco, California with his wife Stephanie and daughter Amelia. He can be contacted at bjaneshak@sbcglobal.net or 714-777-2500

**Ishwari Jay** is an author, speaker, entrepreneur, and Anusara yoga teacher. She has spent the last decade empowering thousands of people to reach their full potential. Born in France, she studied acting and became a successful actress and model at a young age. Yet, she didn't find true fulfillment in her life. At 21, she retired from her worldly life and began to fully dedicate herself to her spiritual journey immersed in meditation and intense spiritual disciplines, living in many ashrams (spiritual community) all over the world, including two years in India. She moved to NY in 1996 and became a consultant and a coach in holistic lifestyle & yoga, teaching others how to align with the universal laws and principles to manifest anything they desire. Ishwari is also an Internet marketer and entrepreneur, and founder of www.internetmarketingnationalagency.com and www.conscious-mindful-living.com.

**Dwain A. Johnson** is a seasoned Real Estate Investor, and Real Estate Wholesaler in the Greater Phoenix Area. Dwain's creative Strategies and Alternative Investment Models place him on the cutting edge, in today's rapidly evolving Investment Real Estate Market.

With a focus on Acquisitions, Marketing and Sales, his company, PrimePhoenixWholesaleProperties.com, purchases distressed-asset properties, re-positions those properties, and ultimately re-introduces them back into the residential marketplace, helping to re-vitalize neighborhoods.

Dwain's business thrives in the Phoenix market, where he values his time with his amazing family.

"I'm truly blessed to have the love and support of Julie, my beautiful wife of 25 years; my daughter Jenny, a Cosmetologist; my son-in-law Bill, a Mortgage Broker, who recently completed his first Chicago Marathon; my son Dominic, who is attending College on a Presidential Scholarship, and my youngest daughter Courtney, who is a 3-time National Champion, in Synchronized Swimming."

Prior to a career investing in Real Estate, Dwain served his clients as a Certified Financial Planner, and also as District Manager for American Express Financial Advisors, and SunAmerica Securities.

Learn more about Dwain at:
www.primephoenixwholesaleroperties.com

Dwain can be reached at: dwainjohnson50@gmail.com or 480.620.3683 direct.

**Dan Kravitz** has over 14 years of experience in the financial services industry. He has built his business primarily with entrepreneurs, business owners and individual families. Mr. Kravitz offers comprehensive financial strategies to help his clients achieve financial independence. He has worked to help people prepare for their future, utilizing a consistent financial strategy since 1997. Daniel continues to believe in the principles of hard work, honesty, loyalty and dedication. He understands that while his clients know how to earn money it is his responsibility to help them "make their money work for them." Daniel has held the positions of (OSJ) Office of Supervisory Jurisdiction, (BOM) Branch Office Manager and (BOS) Branch Officer Supervisor and has been responsible for the training and supervision of several hundred agents within his professional career.

Alongside his exciting business life, Daniel greatly values the time he spends with his family and his time volunteering in local church activities. Daniel has been a contributor to the Make a Wish Foundation, the WFG Foundation, All for One Foundation and the Store Front Youth Services. He is an active sports enthusiast involved in mountain biking, wake boarding, weight lifting, off-roading and snowboarding. Daniel's passion, enthusiasm, humor, and knowledge has added value to those who have used him as a business consultant, keynote speaker, and trainer. Daniel lives in San Diego, CA with his wife Linda and their dog Wasabi. Continuing to live within their hearts is their precious son, Dylen Ashton Kravitz. You can find more information at www.dankravitz.com. Daniel can be reached at 619-988-2420.

**J. Massey** is Real Estate Entrepreneur, Infopreneur & Speaker. He is a true living breathing success story in the California real estate market. Starting with less than $0 to his name, he has built a successful investing business that now comfortably supports his and his family's futures. This has all been accomplished with A LOT of initiative and using little to none of his own money or credit. He is masterful at the art of "doing the deal" and problem solving to find win-win solutions for everyone involved. Because of his expertise, he has helped many people build their wealth using retirement plans and real estate. He currently functions as a landlord, lender, consultant, investment manager, speaker, and mentor. You can learn more about J. Massey and how he can help you grow your money faster at www.mrjmassey.com.

**Rosemary Medel** is a city planner for the last twenty years in Southern California. Rosemary has worked for the cities of Huntington Beach, Cypress and Signal Hill. A Bachelor of Fine Arts degree with an emphasis in Environmental Design has prepared her for her current profession in Land Use Planning and Real Estate. Determined to success, she is no stranger to struggle, hardship, and sacrifice. Raised by a single mother, growing up in East LA surrounded by violence and gangs, Rosemary is the oldest girl of six brothers and sisters. Who could imagine this kid from East LA would be so determined to achieve and to find her true voice both as an author and singer? Lead singer in a band and, yes, single mom with two amazing children Rosalie and Eli. She is committed to training and preparing her clients to develop their professional image through improved public speaking and presentation skills, developing self-confidence, and mentoring in professionalism. She has co-author nine books from the Professional Woman Network www.pwnbooks.com a series committed to empowering women and youth.

Rosemary is a certified trainer in Woman's Issues and is an International Advisory Board member of the Professional Woman's Network. She is also a member of The Professional Woman's Network International Speakers Bureau, The Professional Woman's Network and Experts Industry Association. Rosemary is available for personal and professional coaching sessions and gigs to sing. Her most important role and accomplishment has been raising her two grown children Rosalie and Eli. You can contact Rosemary at rosemarymedel@yahoo.com and www.rosemarymedel.com or (562) 556-3636.

**Randy Ngan** is a Real Estate investor that believes in continuous education, personal development and financial education. Randy enjoys helping people who want to help themselves. He has a BA in business finance and learned that usually an academic university does not provide people with the financial knowledge to be financially free. Randy would like to help people by providing financial education to the young and old with a community of local members that will be your mentors and friends. Join the re-knewal process today! Randy can be reached at 619-800-6426 or neighboradder@gmail.com.

**Alia Ott** has a passion for helping others create wealth through investing in companies and projects that make the world a better place. Formerly responsible for leading fundraising programs at Network for Good, Alia's team helped 70,000 charities raise over $530M online and created a system that connects millions of donors and volunteers with causes they care about. Starting at the early age of six when she began her first small business venture, Alia has fully embraced the spirit of a social entrepreneur. Her desire to help others learn how to earn and manage money inspired her to create a financial literacy program for kids called "The Magic of Money." The program teaches youth how to develop smart habits around making, saving, spending, giving and growing money using interactive games and one-on-one coaching.

Alia has spent the last decade investing in real estate and now actively creates opportunities for others to generate wealth through investments in high-performance properties and other types of growth-oriented business ventures. She is the co-owner of investorsinaction.com, a collaborative network of inspired real estate investors and has been fondly named the Chief People Officer of CHARITY INC due to her ability to connect worthy organizations to the resources and funding they need to become sustainable. CHARITY INC is an online and offline cooperative network that incubates, mentors, funds and connects entrepreneurs with investors to develop social enterprises that are self-sustainable, growth-oriented and designed to make the world a better place - our business is GOOD!

To find more information about CHARITY INC visit www.charityinc.org. Alia can be reached through her personal site www.aliaott.com or via email at alia@investorsinaction.com.


**Harry Paul** has a Ph.D. in experience. With over 30 years in business, including running all aspects of management training and consulting business, Harry has first-hand knowledge of everything related to sales, distribution, product development and international operations. He has served as a senior vice president for The Ken Blanchard Companies, where he personally managed the speaking career of Dr. Kenneth Blanchard, co-author of *The One Minute Manager*. Harry is the co-author of six books including the internationally bestselling business book *FISH! A Remarkable Way to Boost Morale and Improve Results. FISH!* has been on the bestseller lists of: The New York Times, The Wall Street Journal, USA Today, Business Week, Amazon.com and Publisher's Weekly and is one of the best selling business books of all time. Harry Paul brings the messages in his books to life in each of his presentations. He has shared his message with hundreds of organizations to help get their people excited about coming to work and working hard; where decisions are based on the Mission, Vision, and Values of the organization. With his easy going and humorous style audiences leave his presentations energized and armed with information to start making a positive difference, immediately. Work Made Fun Gets Done! More information can be found at Harrythefishguy.com.

**James V. Pham** is a Visionary, Entrepreneur, Master Marketer, Social Media Enthusiast, Tea Lover and Expert, Meditation Practitioner who owns several startup companies and whose personal Vision is to help others become more financially rich, free, and secure while sharing Love, Light, and Luxury throughout the world. He is currently the Founder/Chairman/CEO of EnlighTea Café, Inc., ESI, Inc., EVX, Inc., and is a proud Graduate of CEO Space International. James holds two 1st Degree Black Belts, 1 in Tae Kwon Do and the other in Dragon Dance, an original form of mixed martial arts.

With his background in real estate acquisitions, property management, and business consulting; his experience in creating beautiful and uplifting environments; and his extensive experience as a practitioner and teacher of meditation, James is in a perfect position to launch and manage EnlighTea Café and to take the corporation public. For more information contact James at james@enlightea.com, or visit www.enlightea.com.

**Brian Roman** made the life-altering decision in Sept of 2005 to change careers. His decision was a bit unusual as Brian left a conventional career to pursue his dream and passion to become a singer/entertainer. Brian has been performing all his life but never believed it was possible to make a career of it. He mortgaged his home to produce his first CD "As Long As I Have Music" and to stage a career launching concert. Brian booked Canada's premiere concert hall, Toronto's Roy Thomson Hall, he also booked a 17-piece orchestra and a 150-member choir. He then spent six months selling tickets. On April 26th 2006, Brian walked on stage to a sold out crowd singing the impossible dream. The next morning the story of this great triumph was featured on the front page of the largest newspaper in Canada, *The Toronto Star*. In the last 5 years he has played to audiences in Canada, Europe, the Caribbean and the United States. He has performed with some great artists like Rita McNeil, Ronnie Profit, Rich Little, The Bare Naked Ladies and Jose Feliciano. Brian has recorded three CDs and is now working on the forth with his new manager Zack Werner, known best as the tough, earring-baring judge on the hit TV show "Canadian Idol." Brian's voice and stage presence leave audiences feeling thoroughly entertained and his story leaves them feeling inspired. Brian Roman can be reached at brian@brianroman.com.

**Martha Reed** believes the power to heal lies within and from time to time, we need assistance finding answers or clarification, as we can't seem to get them for ourselves. On occasion, we need help understanding our relationships. Every now and then, we need a little direction and guidance when we feel afraid or stuck. Other times we need help in understanding our emotional or physical aches and pains or illness. Sometimes we need INSIGHTS into how we can heal from within. Often just seeing ourselves through someone else's eyes makes the biggest impact. Sometimes we need to connect to our guides and angels so we don't feel so alone. Other times we need words of hope and ways to find them. This is why people sometimes come to Dr. Reed for Intuitive Coaching, Hypnotherapy or Spiritual Guidance.

Dr. Reed has a passion to assist others in overcoming fears and limiting behaviors that have them feeling unsuccessful, unfulfilled, unloved and downright out of balance. She provides insights and understanding of how one's personality, emotional and spiritual energy can lie at the root of the hurting and imbalance. Using her gift as an empath, with clear knowing, she is able to help uncover blocks and barriers that have kept one chained to the pain and kept one from reaching their full potential of health, success, and happiness. If you're searching for answers and insights for moving the blocks and barriers that are dimming your light and casting shadows in your life, she can take you inward with guidance, support, and visionary insight, healing mentally, emotionally, physically, and spiritually. Martha invites anyone to spend an hour with her because she believes you'll find it uplifting, hopeful, thought-provoking, insightful, and life-changing.

In addition to her degree in business, Martha holds a PhD. She is a Certified Hypnotherapist, a Transformational Life Coach and a Spiritual Counselor, and works with energy medicine such as Homeopathy, Reiki, Color Therapy and Flower Essences. As a Speaker/Teacher/Mentor she also hosts numerous webinars on weight loss, stress-reduction and relaxation, and teaches hypnosis as well. She is a co-author in the award winning book *Thinking upside down, Living right side up.* More information on Martha can be found at www.insights-for-life.com. You can reach Martha at Martha@insights-for-life.com and 623 249-5888

**Peter and Jayne Stanyon** knew instantly that making the move from England with their two young daughters 25 years ago to Southern California was meant to be. Peter has the entrepreneurial spirit and love for life. Together they ran a successful flooring business, but their real passion came to light when they founded their not profit foundation Heart to Heart for organ donor awareness after their daughters Kirsty (22) and Hollie (20) passed away in separate car collisions. Insight is everything, knowing that "Adversity can be your greatest teacher" is a valuable life lesson.

As a speaker, author and mum, Jayne's passion is teaching medical professionals, high school students and everyday people how to live life on so many different levels.. You can transform your life when you choose to change.

They have been awarded the #1 short film at the Hollywood Donate Life Film Festival. Jayne can be reached at jayne@heart-heart.com and Peter can be reached at peter@heart-heart.com.

**Lori Taylor** is a social media technologist, radio show host, author and founder of REV Media Marketing LLC. Lori spent the first two decades of her remarkable career as an award-winning direct response marketer working for RR Donnelley, where she crafted one amazingly successful campaign after another from non-profit direct mail fundraising campaigns, where she has helped to raise more than 2 billion dollars for Disabled American Veterans to award-winning branding strategies and marketing promotions for Fortune 50 companies such as Procter & Gamble and Kroger.

In 2009, Lori decided to leave the corporate world and be her own boss, immediately falling in love with the new emerging world of social media. Consumers were one click away, and as a direct response expert, Lori couldn't wait to get the conversation started. Lori has been tearing it up in 2010, launching hugely lucrative campaigns for everyone from non-profit startups like Live Matrix and Elected Face to massive corporate brands such as Microcenter and "COPS", the TV Show.

Most notably, Lori is the primary architect behind the groundbreaking Power of Fear Summit at Pick the Brain, the Internet's #1 motivational and self-development blog. Following the overwhelming popularity of her courses, "30 Days to Thinking Outrageous" and "90 Days to a Better You," (almost 20,000 people have taken them), Lori recently created and launched an online live event called "The Power of Fear Summit", in which world renowned speakers such as Brian Tracy, Les Brown, Rhonda Britten (America's Favorite Life Coach, Oprah Guest and reality TV star), Greg Reid (face of Napoleon Hill's "Think And Grow Rich" Foundation) and Gary Goldstein (Producer of *Pretty Woman*) were featured, just to name a few.

Lori has also worked as a collaborative business partner directly with Tony Robbins, Tom Nunan (producer of *Crash*), Loreen Arbus, Nova Spivack, Sonja Nuttal, Donna Karan, Jane Fonda and many others. Her network seems to be unlimited! She even successfully received a Tom Hanks endorsement at his Facebook page for her most recent online success with her charity Disabled American Veterans, with her "Home OF The Free, Because of the Brave" video campaign which hit the home page of YouTube with over 512,000 views in one weekend.

**Tom Thomson** could best be described as a man who understands hard work, discipline, integrity and the value of doing the right thing. He grew up in a military family of eight kids where hand-me-down clothes were the norm. A decorated veteran, he gave unselfishly throughout his 27-year career to the young men and women serving under him, mentoring them to achieve, and sometimes surpass his own highly successful military career. He enjoys reading everything technical, can fix most things mechanical, and is regularly known to leave even the most aware speechless with his quick wit. Tom has been a foreign car mechanic, an aircraft mechanic and avionic technician, a family financial planner and continues to act as CPMG (chief polisher/master gopher) for his wife's metal-smith business. He would rather spend his time hunting and fishing in Alaska or scuba diving in warm tropical waters but continues to work for Alaska Airlines as a technical trainer. He says his proudest accomplishment is his 39-year marriage to his wife Deborah, whom he met as a result of a blind date. A man of faith who has recently rededicated his life to walking with the Lord, Tom feels a great burden to leave an enduring legacy for our nations children who are floundering without guidance and stability in their lives. Tom can be reached at trtevo@gmail.com or 602-696-9599.

**Brian Tracy** is a leading self development author and coach in the United States of America. Tracy is a best-selling writer with more than 40 books published, more than 300 video and audio programs produced, and a live audience of more than 250,000 each year. "I believe through learning and application of what you learn, you can solve any problem, overcome any obstacle and achieve any goal that you can set for yourself."

Brian Tracy has produced more than 300 different audio and video learning programs covering the entire spectrum of human and corporate performance. These programs, researched and developed for more than 25 years, are some of the most effective learning tools in the world.

Brian Tracy is happily married to his wife Barbara and lives in San Diego with their 4 children.

# Forthcoming Projects by Sherpa Press

## The Rise

Spring 2012

Want more life nuggets?

## Everything is Subject to Change:

### Finding Success When Life Shifts

## Off the Coast of Zanzibar:

### Coming of Age for a Second Time

*Have a story to share?*
Be featured in one of our best-selling titles.

Email **Allyn@sherpapress.com** today and learn how
to participate in an upcoming collaboration.

You can also visit us at: **www.sherpapress.com**